Dateworthy

get the relationship you want

intelligent

open-minded responsible

funny self-aware

Dateworthy

trusting sexy

magnetic

self-respecting

confident

passionate

DennieHughes

RelationTips columnist for

USA WEEKEND

RODALE

Printed in the United States of America

Rodale Inc. makes every effort to use acid-free ∞, recycled paper ♻.

Book design by Tara Long

Dennie Hughes's hair/makeup by Jovan

Library of Congress Cataloging-in-Publication Data

Hughes, Dennie.
    Dateworthy : get the relationship you want / Dennie Hughes.
        p.   cm.
    ISBN 1–59486–075–0 paperback
    1. Dating (Social customs) 2. Man-woman relationships.   I. Title.
HQ801.H935   2004
646.7'7—dc22   2004013385

Distributed to the trade by Holtzbrinck Publishers

2   4   6   8   10   9   7   5   3   1   paperback

RODALE
LIVE YOUR WHOLE LIFE™

FOR MORE OF OUR PRODUCTS
WWW.RODALESTORE.COM
(800) 848-4735

To my Mom and Dad,
for their support and love, and for showing me
what a relationship worth having looks like

To Peter,
for going above and beyond Dateworthy
I.L.Y.M.

To Gina,
my very, very best friend,
Thanks—L.Y.L.A.S.

Acknowledgments

The Dennie Hughes Experience wouldn't be possible without:

Joe Regal—thank you so much for never letting me see *you* sweat! Your never-wavering support, encouragement, and belief in me enabled me to leap tall buildings in a single bound . . . and maneuver smaller ones in blackout situations. Joey Onion, man of many layers—I look forward to many years together.

Carol Clurman, Jack Curry, and everyone at *USA WEEKEND*—thank you, Jack, for bringing me onboard the greatest magazine in the country and much love to Carol, who aids and abets my RelationTips column. Carol, in a word: you *rule*!

Rodale Press for being 110 percent behind the *Dateworthy* vision—I'm ecstatic about being a new member of the Rodale family.

Jennifer Kushnier, who gets especially giant-sized hugs for being so patient, such an enthusiastic cheerleader, so darn talented—and for understanding the importance of a good giggle in between deadlining. I'm glad we were in this thing together.

Mark Liebman—my sixth grade teacher who absolutely was the guiding force behind the path that I ended up choosing . . . and which has ultimately taken me to where I am today.

A major standing ovation to:

Danny—for being so inspiring and full of amazing ideas, for being pushy when I needed it, for all the stress-releasing, cocktail-fueled fun, and, of course, for introducing me to the most amazing agent in the world.

Bess—my reigning Chat Princess.

Lee—for not only giving me my first column, but helping me stretch and grow into a better writer and reporter—your belief in my talents made me believe as well.

And huge hugs for:

My Enlist to Resist team—the grrlfriends who provided a listening ear, a shoulder to cry on, and the "you go, girl!" support, especially the in-it-for-the-long-haulers: Michele Gill Samuels, the fabulous Mz. Trinetta Love Reid, Laurie Pansini, Michele Promaulayko, and Francine Napolitano.

David Robinson—my aisle-guy—and "Team Ratweiler"—I love you guys!

Father Daly and my RCIA group at Our Lady of Peace, for helping me reestablish my relationship with Someone who has always walked beside me through every high and low.

Jaimie, personal trainer extraordinaire—I still can't believe how he buffed the blob out of this bod!

My fabulous female team at Allure Day Spa for the relaxation—and rejuvenation.

All the incredible experts who carved time out of their busy schedules to work with me.

My readers, both at *USA WEEKEND* and USAToday.com— I'm honored to be trusted with your most important questions, thankful for your kudos, and appreciative for the criticisms and suggestions that open me up to a new way of looking at things.

And, of course . . . thanks to every single Good, Bad, and Salvageable Guy for providing me with some great date stories!

Contents

Part 4: Great Date = Possible Mate?

Part 5:
Readers' Most Frequently Asked Questions

Introduction

I've always been an advice person. I can honestly remember sharing some words of wisdom back in kindergarten with my friend Julie, who was trying to decide whether to play with blocks or finger paints. "Blocks," I said, "because you're wearing white, and paint will make you dirty."

As for dating, well, *that* started as early—and came as naturally!—as the laundry advice. My very first day of kindergarten, I was approached by a brown-haired boy in plaid shorts named Etelvino Valdino. He stared deeply into my eyes and demanded, "I want you to be my girlfriend," then ran away to play with the other boys. Fascinated by this new experience, I couldn't stop watching him for a good thirty minutes, trying to figure out if he truly was my boyfriend just because he said so—and if he was, was that a good thing, like Yodels or being on the swings? When he got into a fist-fight with another boy who made fun of his short pants (and his long name) and was made to stand in the corner as punishment for his actions, I decided right then and there that yes, I would absolutely be his girlfriend. After that first day, we held hands every time we lined up to walk down the hall to the bathrooms and shared the snacks our moms put in our lunchboxes until his family moved away. Sigh.

It's been a long and interesting road from finger paints and sharing Drake's Cakes with boys in short pants to the very pressing, personal problems I get as the RelationTips columnist for *USA WEEKEND* and during my live chats at USAToday.com. Over the last four years, I've received thousands of letters from readers who are either at the end of their ropes or ready to tie one around the neck of someone they are just not relating to. The questions I am asked—especially the dating questions—are touching, disturbing, intimate, and sometimes downright humorous. What hasn't changed is that, just as I did for Julie, I answer each question as personally, empathetically, and directly as possible.

Everyone wants to be a part of a couple, to be loved and be in love. People understand that dating is a necessary evil on the road to achieving this kind of happiness—but have no clue how to begin the process or what to look for in another person. The idea of baring their hearts (especially if they've been burned a few times) or of dealing with the new dating rules (especially for those who are just reentering the scene) is daunting. Faced with one failed relationship after another, many give up on finding true love, never realizing that perhaps the common denominator in all these relationships is their own technique.

That's why I wrote this book. My goal is to help you recognize whether it really was the *other* person who wasn't worthy—or whether it's *you* who needs to work on your relationship skills.

The point I want to make: I never gave up hope, and neither should *you*! The motto? Crash and burn? Live and learn, baby—let's move forward!

intelligent **Part 1** responsible

open-minded

funny *self-aware*

Oops—It *Is* You!

trusting sexy

magnetic *self-respecting*

confident

passionate

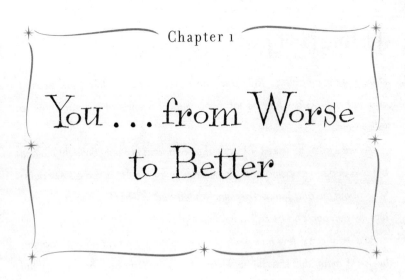

Chapter 1

You ... from Worse to Better

I know you've heard, "It's not you, it's . . . *me*."

And I know you believed it.

But if you've heard that line way more than you've ever heard, "I'm crazy in love with you," it's time to start wondering if perhaps it *could* very well be you. Because, let's face it, the common denominator in all your failed relationships is . . . well . . . *you*!

I'm not saying that you are fully to blame for the end of every relationship. I am, however, saying that you are *fully responsible for the fact that the relationship began in the first place.* You either chose to go after the guy or allowed yourself to be caught by him. Now, I'm the first to agree that there are some guys who are so slick in their presentations that they can fool you some of the time, but when you find you're getting fooled *most* of the time, you ought to take a look at that fabulous female in the mirror and ask, "What, already?"

Dating Diary

Danny was amazing. Tall, dark hair and skin, electric blue eyes. I couldn't believe it when he left his group of friends at the car show to talk to me.

As we spoke, he asked if I wanted a soda, and not only brought me one but also popped it open and stuck the straw in for me. He asked a lot of questions about me and seemed genuinely interested in what I had to say. I gave him my number, and he called me that night.

We went out a few times—in my car, because he said he was loaning his to his mom until she got hers fixed. I was thrilled about how thoughtful he was. I decided I wanted to surprise him one night with a picnic basket for two, which is when I realized that since I always picked him up at work, I didn't actually know where he lived. I took a quick peek into his wallet when he was pumping my gas, looking for his license so that I could

And then, resolve to do something about it.

The first step? Figure out what your dating style is. The only way you're going to stop attracting the wrong types—and get the right ones to stick around—is by recognizing and rejecting some of the bad dating behaviors you've picked up over the years. Here are what I call the top ten most-bound-to-be-broken-up-with behavior types:

+ **The Time Bomb:** Your biological clock is ticking so loudly, you view every first date as a potential rehearsal dinner. You de-

write down the address, and came across some pictures of him posing with a bride . . . and then with kids. When he got back in the car, I asked him about them.

He sighed and said, "Well, I guess I should tell you that I'm married. But I'm not happy, and I only stick around for the kids, you know? I date all the time."

Figures. Mr. Considerate turned out to be Mr. Dad—taking care of the needs of others was second nature!

I was furious, and told him so. I stormed out of the car. He called after me, and I turned around, opting to make a scene. "Screw you. I never want to see you again!" Everyone who was pumping gas or exiting the 7-Eleven watched. I turned to make my dramatic exit when he yelled,

"Hey! Where are you going? This is your car!"

mand to know where the relationship is headed so early and often that he's headed out the door.

+ The Shadow: You may be an independent spirit around your friends, but once you get with a guy, you lose yourself in him. You take on his hobbies; give up everything that's yours to blend in with his life; never express your own point of view, thinking that agreeing with him 100 percent will please him. Disappearing into your guy, however, does not stop him from doing his own disappearing act.

+ **The Drama Queen:** You figure that anything worth having has to be fought for. You shop at Bad Boys R Us, and your favorite way to kiss is during make-up make-outs. You're so busy catching him in lies and trying to be the woman who is woman enough to change him, you haven't even noticed that you are the only one calling.

+ **The Diva:** Your standards leave most men in the "not worthy" category. Many men will try, but only a loser would stick around to be treated like a loser. Inevitably, you end up Queen of Queens (my preferred terminology over "Fag Hag"), because only gay men can tolerate your fabulousness.

+ **The First Sighter:** If you aren't feeling a flash of love and lust within the first moments you set eyes on each other, you don't pursue him any further. Most men will not tread past the "I'm just not attracted to you that way" signs you post immediately.

+ **The Rescuer:** Like the Statue of Liberty, your arms are open to accept the tired, the poor, the downtrodden, and the hungry. Artists and musicians, damaged men who cry . . . you're pretty sure that by being everything to these men, you'll get to heal and keep one. Yet time and time again, they steal your heart, your energy— maybe even your grocery money—and move on.

+ **The Other Half:** Your motto: Any relationship is better than none. You hop from relationship to relationship, never feeling like a whole person on your own, always ready to go steady, even if it means lowering your standards (causing even your closest friends to wonder, "What was she thinking?"). It usually takes guys a few months to figure out that the reason they're not comfortable with you is because you're not either.

+ **The People Pleaser:** The man you date is essentially the man everyone else thinks is worthy. If your parents want him as a son, or if friends you're trying to impress say he's a great catch, then you push your own feelings out of the way. Eventually, he catches on and finds intimacy elsewhere.

+ **The Money Honey:** Love is grand, but several hundred grand is what makes your heart pump faster. You're willing to play by his rules and sell your soul if it means a lifetime of luxury. Unfortunately, being bought leaves you in the powerless position of being sold out once he sees a shinier, newer toy he wants to play with.

+ **The Green Monster:** Your mantra: Men Are Dogs. Your mission: to put a leash on your guy and only allow enough slack to keep an eye on him. Your motivation: You will not be the last to know when he cheats on you. Your man: He won't cheat because he's just loosened the noose and vamoosed!

RelationTip: It's hard to evaluate yourself in love. When you're ready to figure out your part in dating disasters, ask several trusted friends to give you their opinions about what they've witnessed in your past relationships.

Recognize yourself in one of these?

I'm betting you probably cross over into more than one type—I know that I have visited all but one category (you'll just have to guess which one!) during my dating years.

If you find that you do relate to some of these types, know that you're in good company, and these choices are not always your fault. Very often we choose to exhibit certain behaviors because:

+ We're carrying some big, heavy baggage from one or more previous relationships.

+ We model our own behavior on that of our parents (the first "love relationship" we ever witnessed), which, as the divorce rate indicates, was probably not so perfect.

+ We grew up watching soaps and, not knowing how else to act with a guy, adopted a favorite character to try out on boys. Some of us chose the long-suffering nice girl route, while others believed that every man wanted an Erica Kane type. (It didn't matter in the world of daytime television, where *everyone* had at least six gorgeous weddings!)

In the end, though, it doesn't matter why we're acting like bad daytime players—what matters is that we can recognize and change our dating styles.

First, by sending a wake-up call to each personality so that you can actually understand the error of those ways.

Second, by making a checklist of the dos and don'ts of choosing a person who won't drive you back into those bad behavioral patterns. After all, if you don't know what qualities are essential, then how can you not help but repeat history—and histrionics?

Wake-Up Calls
(Or, Why You Should Stop Doing That!)

You've got the information. Now, your mission—should you choose to accept it—is to ditch those most-bound-to-be-broken-up-with behavior types and replace them with your very first Date-worthy actions.

My advice: Read through the wake-up calls below with a friend, and don't skip any. I know you thought you recognized yourself in perhaps only four out of the ten most-bound-to-be-broken-up-with-behavior types, but I'm betting there are bits and pieces of other behaviors that you may not realize—and your friend can actually point out and say, "Oh, are you kidding me? You *always* do that!" (Don't despair—make this a double-Dateworthy challenge, and enlighten her as to her darker dating side.)

Diffusing the Time Bomb

It's not only that most guys can instinctively pick up on the scent of relationship desperation. Demanding to know what the future holds early in a relationship before you even know that the guy is worthy of your love and attention could end up placing you in a "be careful what you wish for" situation, aka, "How do I get rid of Mr. Wrong now that I've led him to believe I wanted to grow old with him?"

Your mission possible: From now on, the words "Where is this going?" do not leave your mouth until you have dated for at least six months. That way, you've gotten past the three-month everyone's-on-their-best-behavior waiting period, and you've started to see his true colors.

Shaking the Shadow

The reason your man *became* your man is because he liked *you*—your conversation, your values, the way your brain and personality work. The more you become a clone instead of a complement to his personality, the quicker he'll become bored and seek out a girl that reminds him of . . . your former self.

Your mission possible: If you need to be reminded of what it was about you that attracted him on those first few dates, *ask him.* And then, every time you're tempted to stifle an opinion, remember his words and speak out!

RelationTip: The best way to initiate a "let's talk" moment with a guy is without the "let's talk" announcement, and during a meal. Never try to get into his head while he's watching TV, or during something sexual, when he's apt to say anything just to shut you up.

Dethroning the Drama Queen

Constant bickering may make for great television, but it's definitely not healthy in a relationship. Life is tough enough, and there are plenty of people out there who are more than happy to give you a hard time. Your man should be the one person you can count on to make you feel good at the end of the day. Fact: Fighting is a great way to avoid being intimate with someone. That said, be honest: Do you do it because you don't know how to open up about what you really need? Did you grow up witnessing drama and are now worried that a steady, happy relationship means there's no passion?

Your mission possible: As you work on those issues, try something new: Make your next relationship one that starts off not as a passion but as a friendship, so that you already know that there's a built-in communication level. That means put the fizzle in the sizzle, baby, and take a second look at guys you keep la-

Dating Diary

. . . I had heard that Bobby was down on women because he had a girl-friend who had hurt him very badly years ago. I decided I'd be the one to heal him, and pursued him wholeheartedly. When he stood me up to be with his friends, I got angry. But then he'd apologize, saying his old girl-friend never let him go out with his friends, and that he figured I was dif-ferent. When we ended up sitting around his house watching TV instead of going out to dinner because he blew his budget on some tech toy or sporting event, he made it all better by saying it was so nice to have a girl (unlike his former girlfriend) who didn't pressure him to be out all the time. At the end of two months, I realized I respected his ex-girlfriend a whole lot more than him and bailed.

beling as "too nice." You'd be surprised at how passionate you can get over someone who goes out of his way to drop off chicken soup when you're sick or who compliments you on your worst hair days.

Downsizing the Diva

It's important to have standards about how you should be treated, but not when it means making another person totally compromise and demean himself. The more you learn to appreciate what a guy does for you instead of criticizing it, the more often you'll see him looking for new ways to make you happy.

Your mission possible: Every time you make an unreasonable demand, stop and ask yourself, "Would I do that for him?" and

"Would I let him treat me like that?" If the answer is no, then you absolutely must rethink your demand—at least, if you want to find a man who doesn't have serious "beat me, whip me" issues. You need to abandon the idea that making a man crawl is worth anything beyond a funny girls-night-out story. When setting standards, make them about mutual respect.

Refocusing the First Sighter

Just one look and . . . that's all it took, right? C'mon now. Can you really base a commitment (let alone a credit-card-busting wedding) on Cupid's invisible arrows or love-energy vibes that transfer through your eyes? Believing in love at first sight not only rules out guys you may find a spark with by spending quality time together, but it also absolves you of having to work too hard on the relationship (hey, if forces beyond your control put you together, then they must be capable of making love disappear too, right?).

Your mission possible: Next time you click with someone from across the room, do go over to say hello, but not before you give that interesting guy you were just talking to your number. As for the stories from couples who say they "just knew" he or she was "the one" from the moment they met, I respond, "That's just what Billy Bob and Angelina Jolie said!"

Rescuing the Rescuer

Be honest. Behind all that sweetness and caring is a woman who wants to be worshipped and appreciated for all her sacrifice. Unfortunately, you're dealing with men, not stray animals. (When will we ever stop comparing men to dogs? My dog has never been disloyal to me!) Most real men want to feel like they can take care of themselves, and their women. . . . Well, they may accept a woman taking care of them, but when they get on their feet, they'll want a woman who hasn't seen them at their worst. Fact: Men who live off their women without paying rent, who borrow money and cars, who are willing to watch them leave for work in the morning while they sit around being "creative," are men with a gigolo agenda and are not worth your time.

Your mission possible: Make a commitment to yourself that the next time you start a relationship, the man has to have as much going on as you do in your life. The more you respect yourself, the more he will respect you.

Making the Other Half Whole

If you're truly interested in having a real relationship, then you must spend some quality time building up a relationship with yourself. (Get your mind out of the top bedroom drawer already! Getting to know you doesn't necessarily mean getting to know what makes you "*Ooo!*" It means that you need to figure out what it is that you want and need from life to be happy on your own and then, using that as a blueprint, to think about what you want someone to bring to that world to enhance it.)

Your mission possible: Make a commitment to spend one month—just 30 days—avoiding hook-ups, instead concentrating on what you like to do, whether it's reading, spending time with friends, or finally figuring out exactly what that stove is for in your kitchen (I'm still working on that one). Take this month to pamper yourself, indulge in things that interest you, and be aware of what makes you happy. On the 31st day, with all this self-awareness fresh in your mind, sit down and make a list of what you deserve from a boyfriend (love, respect, the willingness to get up in the middle of the night to find a 24-hour drugstore when you're sick). Then, make a list of the last five or six guys you dated and see if any of them even comes close to matching that first list.

Don't let this wake-up call make you feel like you've wasted valuable time. Instead, allow yourself to feel fantastic that you devoted time to redirecting your energy. Put your "What I Want from a Boyfriend" list in a place where you're always bound to be reminded by it.

Purging the People Pleaser

It's always helpful to date a guy who your parents and friends actually think is worthy of you. However, if you don't start basing your choices on something more important—*your* feelings—your relationships will be doomed to fail. They may not realize it immediately, but most guys eventually figure out when a woman is just going through the motions. Think about how awful you would feel if you found out that a guy you cared for deeply was only around to make his mommy happy. It's time to put your feelings ahead of everyone else's opinions.

Your mission possible: If you meet a guy you like, shove thoughts of "mom would hate him" right out of your head. As a matter of fact, do not introduce any guy to your family or friends until you are sure that he means enough to you that you'll stand up for the both of you. In the end, you'll know who truly has your best interests at heart—the family and friends who are simply happy that *you're* happy.

Closing Out the Money Honey

If you're like most Money Honeys, you already know that dating based solely on the size of a man's wallet is a huge gamble. You'll also probably not care until you are slightly older and realize that the competition for the rich dudes is looking a whole lot fresher than you do. For those of you who are tired of the bling flings, I encourage you to have a different view of what success is.

Your mission possible: Look for the guy who loves his job, has a really great work ethic, and doesn't make money his calling card because he has so much character that he doesn't have to. Besides—in a shaky economic climate, there are no guarantees that the millionaire you met this afternoon won't end up on the unemployment roster two days before your wedding.

Conquering the Green Monster

Been there, and it's ugly. It's time for you to drop out of the dating pool and allow your trusted friends and family members (and, in extreme cases, counseling) to help you put the past behind you.

Your mission possible: First, let them know you're ready to approach dating in a different way and encourage them to give you a short list of things they think are terrific about you. Then, ask friends who have seen the guys who put you through the wringer help you identify the type you usually go for; being aware of normal patterns is your first step toward breaking them. Finally, as you ease back into the dating scene, take steps to make sure the relationship progresses slowly. If the relationship feels like it's becoming serious, you absolutely must find some time to sit down and tell him that you sometimes have trust issues, but that you are working on them and hope that he will understand when you sometimes question things he does. I did the very same thing with my husband when we were dating. He later told me that knowing how I felt, he found himself being that much more thoughtful when considering blowing off a call or going out with the boys.

✦ RelationTip: If you start talking about future plans and your man changes the subject, he's sending a message you should pay attention to—even if you don't want to.

What Matters
(And Things You Thought Did That Don't)

Recognizing your behavior patterns is a great start on the road to knowing what makes you Dateworthy. Now that you know yourself a little better, it's time to start scoping out what makes a *guy* Dateworthy. Love—and lust—is blind, so here's a seeing-eye guy guide to start your quest for (as perfectly said in that immortal rock classic) a lover who won't drive you crazy.

The Non-Negotiables

The Non-Negotiables are the absolute, bare-bones, essential character traits every guy you date must have. It's the gold medal standard of the Dating Olympics, and before you even contemplate a second date, he must score at least a 9.9 (perfect 10 would be great, but you know how the French judges are).

He's honest. Without honesty, there's no *trust*, which is the foundation of every successful relationship. The last thing you want to do is be with a guy you feel you have to keep tabs on 24/7, or worse . . . who drives you to do things like check through his wallet and pockets because he's got a history of not telling the truth . . . particularly the whole truth.

He's loyal. If he isn't loyal to friends and family, you can bet he isn't about to change for the better for you. A guy who knows how to be loyal—a quality that means he can be counted on to stay true to things he's committed to—often knows how to be emotionally and sexually exclusive.

He respects you. When a man respects you, very often it's because he appreciates and shares your values and ethics system, which is crucial to relationship compatibility.

He contacts you regularly. Know that feeling you get when you are mad for someone and where almost everything reminds you of him? Same thing for a guy, and in this day of cell phones, text messaging, and e-mails, the only real reason for not hearing from him is simply because you were not on the brain—or in the heart.

The Negotiables

The Negotiables are the things that are important but aren't absolute, set-in-stone requirements. They are traits that will enhance your compatibility but also leave a little bit of breathing room with respect to interpretation. For example, you and he both have different ideas about what makes for a "comfortable living." That's a positive Negotiable issue that both of you can work through. On the flip side: You and he both have different ideas about saving money—you do, he doesn't. This becomes a negative Negotiable . . . and for me, one that, unless he's willing to get some credit counseling, I'm not willing to take a chance on.

Here are the Negotiables for you to consider:

Education. You're Ivy League, he's strictly community college. But while some of your stuffy friends may look down their noses at his lack of degree, getting through school was a chore for you; he, however, reads the classics and the *New York Times* because it's fun. What's key here is that you are intellectually matched to the point that you get each other's jokes and can discuss and debate current events with each other and socially.

Finance. You want to be in the corner office, he's content to make his money at a lesser-paying job he loves with minimal stress. While you may think it's important to have someone who is just as ambitious as you are, what's truly the key financial issue is that you share similar ideas of how to spend and save.

Cultural/religious beliefs. You don't have to be the same ethnicity, color, or religion (although your family might disagree); not sharing the same cultural background should not be a major concern. Sharing a mutual respect for each other's customs, however, and a willingness to share those traditions, should be. (This is especially true when it comes to children. It's imperative to be direct about any Non-Negotiable issue with regards to raising the children a certain way—for example, in the Catholic Church—in this otherwise Negotiable topic.)

The Non-Essentials

The Non-Essentials are the things that many women find attractive but are only as important as deciding whether you agree with *People* magazine's newest pick for Sexiest Man Alive. If it's not listed among the Non-Negotiables or Negotiables, it shouldn't be your top consideration when deciding whether someone's Dateworthy. Here are the top three, however, that a huge percentage of my female readers seem to fall for every time.

He's a great dresser or dancer. I can't believe how many letters I've received where it's the first thing a woman mentions about why she went out with a man. (No wonder John Travolta continues to be such a phenom!)

He's an incredibly hot commodity. Far too many women base

Dating Diary

Chris was this gorgeous hunk I was stark raving mad about. I gave him my number at his part-time job at the hardware store (I scrawled a note that I attached to a can of Coke. I knew he always had one at noon.) He said he'd try to call and didn't; I called him at home later, and he was sweet and apologetic, saying he hadn't had a chance to call but was going to later. I kept calling each following day until my mother finally intervened.

"Why are you making excuses for his not calling?"

"Well, because I know that if he didn't like me, he wouldn't be so nice when I did get him on the phone."

"He's nice because his mother taught him right. Think a second. You know how there are boys who call here and you tell me to tell them you're not home? And then you never call them back, and if they catch you on the phone, you're very sweet and have an excuse why you didn't call? And then, if it's a guy you're crazy about, you always find a way to call back?"

I said nothing. I knew where this was going.

"Well," she continued, "When you really, really like someone, you always make time in your day to talk to them."

I used to hate it when Mom was right. I still do. But I'm smart enough to know good Portuguese wisdom when I hear it.

---

their self-worth on bagging the cutest or the richest guy in the neighborhood.

He cooks. Think it's only men who have a direct path to their hearts via their stomachs? Guess again. Women are nurturers; they think that a man who cooks is not only sensitive and caring, but that he'd make a great dad. Reality check: That your man knows his way around a stove is a great perk, but his first qualifications for filling the job as your significant other should be skills such as honesty, loyalty, and respect!

Guess what? You've just completed your very first baby steps taking you from "worse" to so much better. So let's recap:

1. Yes, it was *you* . . . sort of. It was the worst of you brought out by the worst of past choices.

2. Recognizing the worst is the first step to making it better. The worst of you can be rectified once you recognize it.

3. Knowing the important Dateworthy qualities to look for in a guy will allow you to make the best of choices and bring out the best in you.

But we've only just begun! Let's take a look at other changeable "It's *you*" behaviors that we can fix, working toward the goal of knowing that when he says, "It's not you, it's . . . *me*," you'll have to agree!

And know what I think you're going to love the most? The work ahead *isn't* full of all kinds of confusing psychological dating double-talk. It's straightforward, from the trenches, lived-it-and-learned-it-because-I-wasn't-in-grad-school-but-dating-up-a-storm stuff that I think will be easy to immediately implement in your dating toolbox.

Full speed ahead!

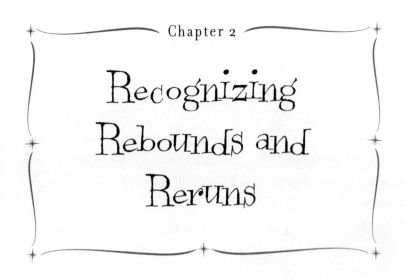

Chapter 2

Recognizing Rebounds and Reruns

So, you've figured out that you're a straight-up Diva. Or perhaps the more common Time Bomb–First Sighter (your first instinct: he's definitely the one; your second date plan: lunch . . . at some restaurant with a view of the Vera Wang bridal design studio).

Good for you, girlfriend. It's never easy to acknowledge an "It's *you*" behavior, but it's an absolute necessity if you want to get on the road to Dateworthiness. And while many of you—especially you Drama Queens—may be tempted to use this knowledge as your ready-made, woe-is-me card ("Oh, well, I've come to the conclusion that love will pass me by, because, after all, I've got severe Shadow leanings."), don't. This is a *light bulb* moment: shedding light on your undateworthy behavioral tendencies makes them easier to spot before they get in the way of halting a potential relationship in its tracks.

Your next challenge is to recognize—and reject—the two easiest relationship traps to fall into: rebounds and reruns.

Rebounds

You shoot for a winning relationship . . . you score! No, wait! You missed. Instead of scoring, you smacked into the backboard and, like it or not, you've landed with a thud right back in the singles game.

The rebound. Whether you're the newly minted rebounder or the unlucky soul who catches someone who is himself rebounding, the dynamic is the same: Only one of you in this relationship is ready to be involved. The rebounder is *not* in it to win it for the team, but for more selfish reasons: to keep from feeling lonely and to boost broken-down self-esteem issues. You know that saying, "Misery loves company"? It's only half true: Misery *needs* company to move forward, but love—well, love has nothing to do with the company that gets mixed up with the miserable.

Rebound Recognition

Recognizing the rebound in yourself—and in someone else—isn't an easy thing to do. As a matter of fact, just *because* you are at your most vulnerable during this time (and the need to fill in that empty spot in your heart is so overwhelming), it's hard to make yourself stop feeling—and start thinking. So let's get right to it before you pull a Jennifer Lopez. What follows are the top rebound red flags to help you know whether *you* are in rebound mode.

You have ex-rated fantasies. Dreaming about getting back with—or at—your ex is the number one indicator that you lack quality space in your heart or head for someone new.

Dating Diary

After I caught Jazz cheating on me yet again, soon after I had forgiven him, I immediately jumped into a relationship with Sam.

Sam . . . had a great Trans Am. And he was very cute and had been pursuing me for ages. We didn't really share any of the same interests, but I really liked getting out—and making sure we stopped at places where I knew Jazz would be so that he could see me.

He saw me, all right. And one night he was so drunk, he threw a glass at us. And Sam said, "You know, I really like you a lot, but . . . not enough to be in the line of fire." And I actually told him that if he didn't think I was worth dealing with danger, he could go. And he did.

At the time, I was so convinced that my showing off had everything to do with being extremely happy to be with this great guy . . . when, truth be told, I shouldn't have gone anywhere near a new guy until I got over the old.

You're too quick to commit. A willingness to immediately commit body, mind, and soul to the first few guys who pay attention to you after a breakup is classic rebound-recharge behavior. You are using their attention as a way to make yourself feel better.

Take out takes on new meaning. If you take out your frustrations and anger on every man who takes you out and find you are making every new guy pay for your ex's crimes, you are not ready to be dating.

Now, how do you spot if *he* is in rebound mode?

Every sentence starts with X. If he cannot stop talking about her, he's not over her.

He knows your schedule better than you do. If he's got to know where you are every minute of every day, you can bet it's because he's lost what every good relationship needs to be based upon: trust.

He wants you to reveal what he won't. Your man is constantly asking you how you feel about him, revealing nothing about his own feelings for you. Typical man behavior? Possibly. Or it may be the typical rebound-recharge—what matters to him is hearing that he's man enough to make you fall for him. Either way, the guy who doesn't feel the need to make you feel needed is, well, *not* needed.

Finally, how do you avoid being—or causing someone else to be—a rebound statistic?

Start by understanding that the end of a relationship is really the end of a life force that was created and lived by two people. It's the death of a dream for one or both participants. Like getting over any death, you really must allow yourself to go through some grieving stages for the relationship in order to move forward and past it. Whether you've been dumped—or have been the dumper—prepare yourself for four stages of ex-expiration:

+ Denial (you don't want to believe it's over);

+ Depression (yeah, like I've got to explain that one to you and that Häagen-Dazs container);

+ Anger (being mad that he broke up with you . . . or that you ever cared);

+ Acceptance (it's done—what have you learned from this?)

Stage One: Denial

For the dumped: I know you thought things were going so well. They weren't for him, however, and now it's over. During this stage, you'll fantasize and fight for your right to get back together. You may even find yourself in a really ugly place, willing to beg and stalk to get him back. Now is the time when you absolutely need to Enlist to Resist. This is a strategy that calls for your getting some trusted, caring friends and family members in place whom you can call or instant message to help you resist giving in to those and other destructive urges (including heading out in your pajamas to load up on junk food).

RelationTip: To conquer that "I must call or visit him" feeling you may have, take out your calendar or date book and write out an "appointment" to see him first thing tomorrow. You'll calm yourself for the moment knowing you can see him the next day. The next morning, you'll be rested and strong enough to cross it off your calendar.

For the dumper: Believe it or not, doing the deed does not discharge you from denial. What happens here is that you second-guess yourself, *especially* if you hear about or actually witness your ex holding hands with a girl who you may feel is the total upgrade of you.

When you are going to be the dumper, you have the advantage of knowing ahead of time that there will be tough times ahead, so you should Pre-Enlist to Resist. First, make a list of all the reasons why the guy you plan to stop dating was completely undateworthy. Next, supply that list to everyone who you think will be on your on-call-for-support roster. Finally, encourage them to read this list to you every time you have a long night spent alone—to keep you from feeling so desperate for company that you end up going back to what was essentially a bad habit.

Stage Two: Depression

For the dumped: You've realized that yes, he really did kick you to the curb, and you wonder, "How could this have happened to me?" Big hugs to you, sweetie. I know how hard it is to have a broken heart, to feel like you weren't pretty enough or smart enough or just *someone he wanted* enough. It hurts so bad that you cannot believe you will ever, ever feel confident in your ability to be in a relationship again.

This is the time when you will be at your most vulnerable for the rebound, the temptation to leap into another relationship as quickly as possible. The need to get involved with someone who will compliment you, make you feel beautiful or desired, to override the feeling of rejection is extremely powerful. This moment is where your Enlist to Resist frontline of friends and family really pays off.

RelationTip: Grief shared is grief diminished.

Let them help you find things to do on your now-open weekends. Talk about how you feel, but don't forget to listen to them when they tell you their stories of the times when they got through the feelings of desertion and rejection you are facing. Don't be ashamed to allow them to pump up your ego with their thoughts about why you are truly a great catch. And remind yourself that with friends and family who are this concerned about you, you are *so worthy* of someone else's love, respect, and devotion.

Dating Diary

When I broke up with Mitchell, it was with complete confidence that he was so not Dateworthy. That was, until I saw him with Felicia, who was one of those popular girls with perfectly winged hair who sprouted breasts before any of us were out of training bras. At that moment, I spun into a spiral of self-doubt: If she likes him . . . and she can have anybody . . . did I perhaps miss something? Could he have been the love of my life, and I just didn't wait long enough to see it?

I worked at a Hallmark store then and used my discount to send him funny, flirty cards. I called him just to tell him I was thinking about him. I bought Alice Cooper albums (not a fan, but Mitchell was) and quoted some lyrics in notes I left in his locker.

Fachrissake, had I put this much work into math, I might've gotten better than a 68, but I digress . . .

So, I got him back. Took him away from the fabulous Felicia. He was all mine.

Yup. Got back the smoker-breath, the blaring Alice tapes in the car ("Whaddya mean turn it down? You can't listen to a genius with the music down."), the racial jokes.

I ended it. Felicia forgave him.

Wow . . . she took that back?

Perhaps I saw more of an upgrade than there really was.

This is definitely not the time to analyze what you did to contribute to the end, but to nurture your mind, body, and spirit. Now is the time to remind yourself that the package that is you—your looks, your mind, your accomplishments, your sense of fun—isn't what caused the breakup . . . rather, what changed was what *he* needed in the relationship.

For the dumper: Who would've thought that you would've missed all those things that irritated you to the point of wanting to scream? Or that, for some reason, you actually cannot remember why you thought you'd be better off without him? Or worse . . . guilt or uncertainty because being on your own feels so darn lonely?

Stage Two is a particularly tough time for the dumper. Sure, you are very aware that after someone dumps *you*, you could be a rebounder. When *you* are the one doing the dumping, however, it's so easy to fool yourself into thinking that since *you* took charge to discharge, you are obviously okay to move on and into another relationship.

That's soooo wrong, *especially* if the reason why you did the dumping is because you were hurt or betrayed.

RelationTip: Surviving depression is all about thriving. As you spend time bonding with friends and getting reacquainted with the activities you didn't have time to do before, you'll find you won't need a romance to revive your spirit.

Let's be honest. "Good-bye" is a sad word. Shakespeare had it right when he had Juliet say, "Parting is such sweet sorrow." It's true—even though you knew the relationship had to end, there is still a lingering sense of unpleasantness or regret that things didn't work out.

Until you have taken a time-out to resolve the whys and what-ifs of your last relationship, the chances that you will be caught up in a rebound situation are almost certain. I'm sure it's easy to grasp that concept if your dumping decision was reached due to distasteful behavior on his part; how, if he lied or cheated or abused you, you are likely to bring all those hurt, distrustful feelings into a new relationship. (Technically, in that case, it's important to recognize that you were dumped before you did the actual dumping.)

What's harder to spot is your potential for rebound behavior when you dumped someone purely based on feelings of, "He's such a nice guy, but not *my* kind of nice guy." It was one of those moments when saying, "It's not you . . . it's *me*," (translation: "You can't help it if I'm bored by you.") made you feel liberated and ready for love, exciting and new.

But here's the trap: Without doing the work of figuring out exactly *what* you need from a guy to not be bored, you'll be rebounding off that Love Boat in no time flat—a waste of your time and his.

Instead of diving into a relationship with someone, now is the time to rebuild the one with yourself, to figure out what the heck moves you and motivates you to fall for someone. It's the perfect time to call up all the friends on your Enlist to Resist team and get their input about what they see as your strengths and good points and what they think you ought to look for in a guy.

Stage Three: Anger

For the dumped: You couldn't believe it was over, and then you dealt with the pain and lack of self-confidence from wondering why you weren't enough for him.

I'm so proud of you that you allowed yourself to experience and work through that heartache. Dealing with it head-on is the only way you can prevent it from twisting and turning into something that will affect your life and decisions down the road.

The good news? You've stopped inflicting pain on yourself and beating yourself up and taking the blame for something that takes *two* to make it right.

The bad news is that once you get past feeling sorry, it's very normal to start getting angry that this nobody dared to break your heart.

Anger is a powerful rebound tool—it makes you jump into a relationship just to show that you can, and very often, it's with someone you figure will make your ex extremely upset. That kind of rebound behavior is not only hurtful to the guy you essentially use, but hurtful to *your* reputation.

To get through this stage, engage your Enlist to Resist group. Let them know that you are in "Why did this happen?" mode, and ask them for help with a get-a-grip project: Ask them to write a Do Not Apply personals ad for you. Their task: to write out an ad that highlights the not-so-great qualities of the last few men you dated. Encourage them to be incredibly honest about what they see are critical characteristics that aren't right for you. Then turn that passion that is currently anger into something productive: determination not to be duped or dumped again. Yes, we both know there's no guarantee that you won't ever be dumped again, but at the very least, most likely it won't be by a guy who fits the Do Not Apply list your friends will help you compile.

For the dumper: If you dumped for any reason other than he treated you despicably, then most likely you won't experience much anger. After the sadness (and some thought process about your

Dating Diary

I had gone through a serious spell of being dumped after two or three great dates, and it was so frustrating. And disheartening. The worst part was that I wasn't even formally dumped—all dating parties involved just disappeared, never to be seen or heard from again.

One night, I was out with my friends when this guy totally caught my eye. I went right up to him and invited him and his friends to our table.

As we all talked, it was pretty obvious to everyone around me that I was all about Ross. My friends tried to warn me that they didn't think he was right for me, but I didn't want to hear it.

We went out a few times. One night we did some serious whipped cream body shot activities. We woke up the next morning, laughing at the terrible stink in the room (now there's a RelationTip for ya: whipped cream + warm bodies + several hours time lapse = yuck). We talked about his picking me up on my birthday the following evening. He left. Never called. I couldn't get a hold of him. My birthday was on an Easter weekend, and all my friends were away. I spent it alone, by the phone, with a turkey sandwich, watching Viva Las Vegas on my 13-inch black-and-white TV.

After I told my friends my pathetic story, one of them said, "Well, we tried to tell you not to date him. . . ."

And I said, "You know what? Telling me not to date him and explaining exactly what it is I need to look for are two different things. Why don't you tell me why you knew he was a jerk?"

And she did. And so did my other two friends. And we started laughing, calling it our "looking for love in all the wrong faces" list.

The next time I met a guy, that night was in my head. And my heart remained firmly off my sleeve.

needs and wants in the next relationship), you'll probably be ready to reenter the dating arena.

However, if you were forced into dumper mode because you were devastated, be prepared that this angry stage could turn you into the very villain you just unloaded. In an effort to regain some sense of control and power over your unresolved hurts, it's the anger—not you—that takes control, leaving you powerless to make very good decisions. The result? You will attract Rescuer types whom you will then walk all over, ultimately losing respect for them and for yourself for becoming a "hurt before you get hurt" kind of person.

Avoid the rebound, tapping into your Enlist to Resist squad. Vent to your friends and family. Let them know how angry you are about how you were hurt. And then ask them to help you write a Do Not Apply personal ad. The more they can list destructive qualities that they've witnessed in past boyfriends, the more empowered—in a positive way—you'll feel to change the course of your dating future.

Stage Four: Acceptance

This stage is also known as, "It happened, but I know I will live to love again." You'll feel that you will live if you lose again. You'll be inspired to put on your mom's old Gloria Gaynor record and dance around and sing at the top of your lungs, "I will survive."

Whether you were the dumped or the dumper, if *you are here*, you are not only ready to explore the dating waters again—you can do so with the confidence that you are out of rebound mode, and that you have learned enough about the rebound to recognize the tendency in others.

At this point, you should definitely include dating in your social repertoire. Just make sure that you take things slowly, and go out without the intention of starting something serious. (The last thing you need is to put your hopes and heart on the line, be rejected, and find your self-confidence plummeting you back a stage.) Go into it with the mindset that you are going to have fun, make a new friend, and have an adventure.

As you explore new relationships, don't forget to keep in mind some of the things your Enlist to Resist group told you with respect to the bad traits of men you have dated . . . so that you can avoid the rerun romance.

Reruns

You know when you date the same kind of guy over and over? When you realize that even though the names and faces change, somehow the story ends up playing out the same?

If so, then it's a sure sign that you are in a syndication situation, or what I affectionately call the Rerun Relationship Rut.

It's very easy to get caught up in the rerun. To once again fall for that guy who stinks at the Non-Negotiables (severely lacking in the ability to be honest, loyal, respectful, or leap tall buildings in a single bound to be with you). You *know* it's a really destructive "It's *you*" behavior, yet . . . somehow . . . like Al Pacino in *Godfather III*, every time you think you're out, you get pulled back in.

I know what you're thinking. Something like, "Well, I can't help it if I have a certain type that I go for . . ." And then, you follow that with an "oh well" shoulder shrug. Maybe even a sigh.

Do you know what I'm thinking?

I'm thinking that until you wipe that shrug and "he's my type" helplessness out of your dating mindset, you will be doomed to cast the same leading man over and over again in your life.

Let's take a look at the two typecasting situations people fall into and how you can grab the controls to cancel those reruns. Think "pilot season," with *you* in the director's seat!

The Physical Factor

You *know* I'm not saying that it's not okay for you to give in to an overwhelming attraction to certain physical characteristics. Whether it's big, beefy boys; bespectacled, gadget geeks; or Latin-lover lookers, we all have that visual something that turns us on and tunes us in to that weak-in-the-knees feeling. As a matter of fact, if certain physical attributes are what it takes to motivate you to take action and make a move to introduce yourself, I say, girl, go for it—and for goodness sake, don't trip on the way over there!

What I *am* saying, however, is that when every guy you date looks like he could be related to your last boyfriend, your friends never introduce you to anyone who doesn't meet your "type" standards, and you walk into a room with blinders on to any guy *except* the usual type suspects, then your physical type "excuse" is, in reality, a bad, very limiting relationship rerun behavior.

There are, however, ways for you to get over your physical typecasting tendencies. To think out of the bias box:

Look for a package deal. Now, stop that. You *know* I didn't mean for you to check out his package. What I'm saying is, instead of focusing on just one physical ideal, make a list of ten visual qualities that you love in order of preference. If he has three out of ten, he gets a shot.

Look with your ears. Yes, women are visually stimulated (hel-*looooo*, Johnny Depp!). But we're also advanced enough to see the

Dating Diary

... Ahhh, Jeff. Blonde, blue eyes, on the football team, and every girl wanted to be his homecoming queen. I didn't much care for his smug attitude, but he was totally hot, and when he asked me out, I pushed aside his constant criticism about what I wore and comparisons with other girls about my looks, and worked hard to live up to my role as his chosen girlfriend. At his request, I never made plans so that I'd always be available when he called. One night, he canceled on me, and, bored, I called up a friend to go out. As we arrived at the bar, I spotted Jeff's car in the parking lot ... and Jeff passionately swapping spit with another girl inside. The worst part? When I walked over, he looked up, said, "You're supposed to be home," and continued the make-out session.

... Ahhh, David. Tall, dark, and handsome, and the local stud legend at the Palms Club. Every girl wanted to be the legend's lady. I didn't care much for his smug attitude, but he was totally hot, and when he asked me out, I pushed aside his constant criticism about what I wore and comparisons with other girls about my looks, and worked hard to live up to my role as his chosen girlfriend. ... Cut to the chase: I took a different route home from work one night, saw his car at a friend of mine's house, stopped by ... Sound familiar? It was the first time I ever saw Twister played that way. ...

... Ahhh, Chris. He was in a band, totally charismatic, so cute that he had a huge female following. Every girl wanted to be the next subject of one of his ballads. ... Yup, you know the rest.

not-so-obvious beauty in a guy who can make us laugh and feel appreciated. The next time a not-your-type guy approaches you with great conversation, listen and look carefully—you may notice that while he doesn't have blue eyes, his brown eyes are still deep enough to get lost in.

Look for a friendship. Very often, visual stimulation makes you get too physical, too fast, and trust me—no matter how amazing someone is to look at across the table, if the only thing he has is gazeability, dating is doomed. If you meet a guy who is awesome to be with and talk to, though he's not necessarily your type, hang out and see what develops. I did that with this dark, 6'5", 275-pound giant teddy bear of a man (sooooo not Johnny Depp), and I ended up with a husband in June 2004!

The physical recast—not too hard to do, and actually . . . kind of fun, when you think about how you've just opened up a whole new world of leading men. Now let's take a look at another, more insidious rerun.

The Intolerant Tolerance

You know you're allergic to dogs, but you still picked up the pup because it was just too cute not to. Everyone else was ordering ice cream cones and you didn't want to feel left out so you went for it, knowing that later that night you'd be doubled over in gastric agony.

You knew it'd make you say "never again," but you went for it anyway, knowing that you've already learned how to deal with the tortuous outcome. When this it-hurts-so-bad-but-feels-so-right-right-now judgment call comes to play with guys, the intolerant tolerance is in full swing.

Most of us know within the first twenty minutes of talking to a guy whether there's something "familiar" about him ("I feel like we've known each other forever already!"). Yet, even as we pinpoint that he has a lot of qualities as an ex that we used to really, really care about, we forget that this was also the ex that caused the most misery. (We also forget that while our butts looked fabulous after losing all that break-up weight, the face in the mirror looking back was sad, gaunt, and haunted—anything but Dateworthy.)

Some of the ways to spot if you're an intolerant tolerance kind of girl:

+ You can immediately identify who this guy reminds you of—and usually, more than one name comes to mind.

+ You see familiar negative behaviors as a challenge, not a threat.

+ You feel comfortable, in a sick sort of way, with the idea that you know this game—and don't need to challenge yourself to want better.

RelationTip: Building up a tolerance for intolerable guy behaviors means allowing yourself to be controlled by a dating situation instead of controlling it.

This type of rerun behavior is actually the scarier of the two. Being able to build up a tolerance for a man's absolutely intolerant—read: Non-Negotiable—actions could mean serious self-esteem loss for you.

And that, my dear, is not something you can easily shrug off. Actually, this calls for shoulders-back, head-held-high, chock-full-o-determination tactics, such as:

Figure out the source. In order to understand why you are drawn to certain guys over and over again, you need to figure out who they remind you of. People often gravitate to what they've known before in their lives. Whether it's an overly critical dad or a needy first love, there's definitely a connection between how you felt about someone important in your life and the way they treated you. Once you pinpoint that person, make a list of their good and bad qualities so that you have a personality checklist you can be conscious of.

Enlist to Resist. As I mentioned earlier, knowing what's bad for you—and choosing to embrace it just one more time—is a bad thing. Now that you're aware, you need to enlist those friends and other forces of good in your life to help you stay strong when you find yourself slipping.

Try the patience diet. If choosing what's good for you all the time was easy, do you think that dieting would be a billion-dollar industry? Healthy dating choices take time, effort, and patience. Understand that you won't be attracted to a new type of guy right away and that the first few times you try to date someone unlike anyone you've ever known (you know . . . respectful, kind, thoughtful, that kind of thing), it's going to feel like you're forcing it. Well, that's because you *are*. It ain't easy to eat healthy after years of junk food. Be aware, be patient, and eventually you will find your tastes changing.

Two of the hardest things to recognize—and reject—are rebound and rerun patterns. However, they are truly key "It's *you*" behaviors that you will need to face head-on in order to establish your relationship readiness—and your ability to be choosier about the choices you make in men.

And speaking of being choosy—let's move on to make sure you get you on board without going overboard!

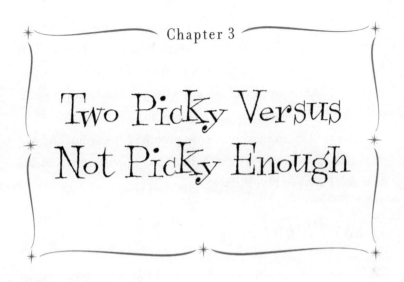

Chapter 3

Two Picky Versus Not Picky Enough

There's nothing wrong with having standards and, of course, a list of Non-Negotiables. Actually, "man planning" is something that every woman should spend some quality time doing before she even considers giving out contact information to a potential love interest. I'd put it right up there with money management.

Think about it: Budgeting in advance—being aware of the differences between what you want and what you truly need—before heading out to shop can help keep you from making one of those crazy impulse purchases you'll regret in the days afterward. (Yes, I've got them in my closet too . . .)

Man planning—like shopping—is about being discriminating, seeking out quality. You are looking for the best buy without sticker (or *ticker*) shock. It's about being . . . Choosy.

I like the word *choosy*. Choosy is about making informed

choices (you know, as in, "Choosy mothers choose Jif"—there's a reason why it's stuck around so long). It implies a certain calm control, where you decide what's best for you based on what you know to be true—who you are and what you have to offer—and what you hope to acquire in a relationship.

Unfortunately, most women cross over the Choosy line and end up in one of two dark, "It's *you*" behaviors: Two Picky (that's Picky² or Picky, Picky) or Not Picky Enough.

Two Picky!

Yes, you do deserve someone who is kind and caring and thoughtful and all-around Dateworthy. The best guy possible. My question, though, is: What exactly does "the best" mean to *you*?

Unfortunately, when many women put together checklists of their ideal mate, they:

+ Fill them with so many Non-Essentials ("must dance well to the beat or beat it, buddy!") that the really important qualities get lost in the listing;

+ Require the kind of insane physical factor requirements ("Brad Pitt abs") that they would deem a man shallow for;

+ Don't truly take into consideration what they themselves have—or rather, don't have—to offer in return.

There are lots of reasons why we feel that sense of entitlement to expect Mr. Not-Just-Right-But-Perfect. Parents. Flicks. Friends who embellish their own love stories to make you feel like they got the full, impossible checklist and then some.

But do you know what I blame the *most* for this?

Dating Diary

Perry was incredibly cute and treated me like the queen I thought I was. When I mentioned that I wanted to see Elton John for my birthday (and that one of my good friends and I were major fans), he got not only us tickets, but two extra for her and her date as well. Afterward, my friend and her guy wanted to go out dancing—a first time for me and Perry. And then . . . it happened. Was he dancing or having a seizure? I was appalled as I noticed other people looking and snickering, and my friend kept giving me the "make him sit down!" look. But there he was, happily oblivious and flailing away to the beat of his own drummer. I decided right there and then that the last thing I needed was a man who embarrassed me on the dance floor. I dumped him and told him why. When the next guy dumped me because my second toe was larger than my first, I realized the ugliness of the Picky list.

Teen fanzines.

Pick up and peruse, and I defy you not to find some picture of a favorite heartthrob with a list of all the *really* important things that would make you his dream girl: "Jesse is a fire sign, so he likes to see his girl in *red*! If you want to be his sweetie, you must be a great bowler! His favorite dish is homemade meatloaf! You're his ideal date if you can belch like one of the guys while still looking girly in a dress and high heels!" Exclamation point, indeed.

From an early, impressionable age, we read this stuff voraciously and compare notes with other girlfriends about who has the most matches on JESSE'S FAVES! list. And then, without realizing it, we started making our own silly, shallow faves list, unconsciously mimicking the celebrity style—an "if I think like one, I will attract one" mentality, if you will.

Now we're walking around with lists of things that we think would make us happy ("No black socks with shorts! Must be able to hold his liquor! Has to vote Republican!") and we're picking, picking, picking away at our potential dating pool until we're down to the last seven guys on earth . . . and of course, four of them are involved with each other.

And the other three . . . well, girlfriend, they are out of your league.

Oh yes, I did say that.

Out-of-Your-League Syndrome

For the Two Picky, there is a severe lack of realization that there are times when you are reaching way beyond your dating zone.

I know what you're thinking. You're absolutely indignant that I would even suggest that some guy is so much better than you that you need not even apply for the job of significant other.

Wrong.

RelationTip: Expect from another only what you expect you have to offer back.

What I am suggesting, however, is that being Two Picky will lead you to believe that the *only* guys good enough for you are the guys who are listed in most eligible bachelor lists, despite the fact that they have qualities and interests that *you* don't possess. And with all probability, those qualities and interests will be exactly what he's looking for in a woman because . . . after all, for him, it's something they will truly have in *common* with each other.

Think of it this way. Let's say you're a star player (you look terrific, you're intelligent, talented . . . a totally terrific package) on a winning team (the people you run with are also top-notch). And you meet another star player on an equally winning team. But . . . you two are in two different leagues that actually have different rules to follow and grounds to play on . . . and you realize that in order to play on that new league, you'll have to adopt a new set of guidelines that you honestly don't feel makes your game better.

My point is that not every perfect guy will be a perfect fit—and trying to make yourself a size 1 when you feel way better in a size 8 is an unhealthy way to live.

That said, here's how to spot when your Pickiness has landed you with someone out of your league:

+ He meets all of your Non-Essentials and physical factors but not one criterion that makes you feel like you have something important in common.

+ Being with him is more stressful than blissful because you feel the pressure of "keeping up" with his world.

+ You start to feel like you're dating him just to prove you can.

+ Girl, you're exhausted.

I know it's possible that you could actually learn to speak seven languages, play croquet, or bone up on classic cars (you won't own any, but you'll know a good one when you see it). And if that's something that interests you, go right ahead. But don't do it because you're Two Picky to date guys whom you rate as undateable merely because they aren't making *everyone else's* lists. Because, after all, that's the kind of "It's *you*" behavior that defines you as a Diva with People Pleaser tendencies, a lethal combination.

Having self-worth—a great thing. Having self-esteem to know that no one is *better* than you—bravo. Being Two Picky because you think that self is better than anyone else—you are definitely sabotaging your Dateworthiness. Would *you* want to be with someone who made you feel like he was just doing you a favor?

Let's take a look at the other side of the dating coin.

Not Picky Enough

When your standards are so low, man planning for you goes something like this: "Guy should have a job. Or at least be looking for one. Or at least have big dreams. He should also brush regularly. Or at least on the nights when he's not too stoned to care."

And then, when he meets one of those expectations, you sigh and think, "I've found my one true love."

I hate to tell you this, but if you manage your money the way you man plan, you're going to end up broke along with broken-hearted.

RelationTip: If you don't believe you're worth more, no one else will.

The Not Picky Enough girl doesn't hold out for perfection like the Two Picky girl. Actually, she's someone who hasn't met an imperfection or Non-Negotiable she cannot rationalize away or completely ignore. Because, after all, she knows she's not perfect—why

Dating Diary

When I acquired my contact lenses and dyed my hair platinum blonde, I was suddenly considered totally hot. Beneath those Clairol roots was an extremely swelled head, and it got to the point where I decided a guy should absolutely prove how lucky he felt to be with me. Thus, every time I was asked to go dancing, I insisted that he buy me a new dress. And, believe it or not, I got my way. All my girlfriends loved telling the tales about how I got stuff without "putting out" and basically had guys being stupid over me.

And then I set my sights on Jake. He was gorgeous, smart, and single. We always smiled at each other when we saw each other out, and we talked just enough to make my heart hopeful. Finally, after weeks of small talk, I asked his sister (a friend of mine), "How come Jake never asks me out?" And she made a face and said, "Oh my God, I like you, but I would never want someone like you to date my brother—I've already told him all about your dating style."

should she expect someone to meet a checklist of qualifications when she herself probably wouldn't measure up?

If you find yourself nodding your head in support of that last sentence, I want you to stop . . . and save that energy for the changes you need to make.

There are a lot of Not Picky Enough reasons why women allow just about any kind of idiot into their lives:

Solo is so lonely. Also known as the "having a bad date is better than no date at all" mentality. You, like Jennifer Lopez, are a chain dater who never learned how to be alone.

Self-worthlessness. Why should you hold out for someone who treats you well when you don't think you're all that?

Ignorance of the law. It's not that you intend to—it's just the way you've always dated. And, most likely, the way others dated around you growing up.

Down from a dump. He dumped you and now you just need someone—anyone—who likes you better than you like him in order to feel desirable—and safe.

Look over at the guy sitting on the couch next to you right now. The one picking his teeth while shelling pistachios all over your new couch. If he's a product of any of the above undateworthy moments, it's time to save yourself and your furniture and get rid of him. Is he gone? Great—the choice you made puts you smack on the Choosy track.

Now that you're fired up and ready to rumble, I want you to take the aforementioned Not Picky Enough feelings and put a new spin on them.

RelationTip: The guy who isn't doing something _for_ you isn't for you.

Flying solo is traveling light. Hanging on to Bad Baggage leaves little room in your life for good luggage. (More on that in the next chapter.)

Self-worth_full_ness. Here's one time when _less_ is not more. Anytime you feel worthless, I want you to stop and write down all the things about yourself that you are proud of: your favorite characteristics, talents, and all the names of the people whom you count as friends and what you admire about them. I want you to keep writing till the page is _full_. Then, read it out loud. My goodness, girl, just

Dating Diary

After a particularly long dry spell, all I wanted to do was find a boyfriend. I gave out my number to any guy who would ask.

Charlie . . . body of Zeus but a face that was nothing to write home about. To me, anyway. If you asked Charlie, he was gorgeous. Somehow, that confidence was . . . attractive. I kept going out with him despite the fact he kept telling me how I could really benefit from fasting for about 30 days. The last straw was when we were out to dinner with his friends, and as I stood up to go to the bathroom, he put his hand between my thighs, tightly gripped the inside of one, and, laughing, said, "No dessert for you!" I should've walked out right then and there. But I came back from the bathroom . . . and didn't have dessert. I didn't get the chance to be angry because he never called after that night.

Daniel was rich. Really rich. He wasn't even 25, and he had a butler and a house with a pool on the water. I loved how money was no object, no matter what we wanted to do. The fun times, however, were only when he was in the mood. I stuck around despite the fact that he wouldn't let me work or leave home when he wasn't with me. He started to do something that was normally a Non-Negotiable for me: drugs. Cocaine, specifically. I pushed it aside because the good times were so much fun. His behavior got more and more erratic and one time, despite my fearful cries to slow down, he pushed his Ferrari to top speed on the highway. I finally got a wake-up call when we were on his boat with another couple—also coke-fiends—and we were nearly killed as he played chicken with another boat. I ended it . . . but still kept in touch, hoping that perhaps I'd catch him the moment he changed.

look at all those things you bring to the relationship table. Why waste them on some schmuck?

Know your rights. You have the right to be treated with respect, care, and kindness and not stay silent when someone is treating you less than you deserve. Anything you say or do should be used to avoid anyone exhibiting Non-Negotiable behavior. And if you sometimes feel like you're too weak to afford to say no to a jerk, your trusted friends and family on your Enlist to Resist team can—and should be—appointed for you.

Resist the rebound. Don't allow a substandard person into your life to distract yourself from a breakup. Remember: The only way to keep a wound from becoming infected is to keep out the germs.

Choosy Is . . . Choicy!

We've explored the Two Picky and the Not Picky Enough pitfalls. Now, ladies, let's discuss out how to get back on the Choosy line.

Choosy, as I mentioned earlier, is that fine line between being unreasonably picky and hopelessly *un*picky. It's about taking control, exhibiting a preference, exercising your option to select someone who you think will be good *with* you—to determine the most Dateworthy guy based not on finding, or excusing, fault; instead, it's choosing based on the positive.

Sounds really promising, doesn't it?

Effective Man Planning

The first thing you should do to kick your plan into high gear is to take stock in yourself. I always believe that if you review history, you don't repeat the bad stuff, and the good stuff stays fresh and new.

Start by going back over the lists you've made so far:

Dating Diary

When yet another guy whom I knew I shouldn't get involved with dumped me, I hit a wall of depression head on. My mom kept asking me what was wrong, and I just shook my head and mumbled, "Nothing. You wouldn't understand." She asked again when I refused dinner that night, but again, I just didn't want to discuss it with her. When I refused dinner the next night (her unbelievable fried chicken, the one I'd reschedule a dinner date for because it was just that good), she had had enough.

"What is it—some boy?" she asked.

"No. Not just 'some' boy. All boys. I don't know . . . I think there's something definitely wrong with me. Boys never want to be my boyfriend."

She thought about it. "Do they want to do things you don't want to?"

"Sometimes," I said.

"So you tell them that you won't, right?"

I nodded.

She shook her head. "Listen . . . the boys you go out with—they want something you don't want to give, and so they leave not because there's something wrong with you. They leave because they know you are right to say no. But that doesn't change the fact that they still want what they want."

Sigh. Another Portuguese wisdom. I knew she was right but didn't say anything. However, she knew she got to me when I grabbed a wing. And then she said,

"You remember something. I did not give birth to half a person. You don't need anyone to make you a whole person."

"Do you have any drumsticks left?" I asked.

+ The ten most-bound-to-be-broken-up-with behavior types to make sure you haven't lapsed back into any of them.

+ Your Non-Negotiables, which, if you'll remember, should include: honesty, loyalty, respect, thoughtfulness, and of course, really important deal-breakers (non-smokers, hygiene, whatever else is critically important to you).

+ Your top ten physical factors, listed in the order of preference (with a note on the bottom, "3 out of 10 nets contact info!").

+ Your Enlist to Resist crew—all those trusted people to whom you can turn in times of trouble.

Next, it's time for you to evaluate what you need versus what you want. Think about why your last five dating ventures went absolutely nowhere, or worse—straight to hell. Some points to consider:

+ Did you stick so close to your Mr. Perfect guidelines that everyone disappointed you?

+ Were you only dating guys who "looked good on paper"—aka "obvious husband material"—instead of finding a friend first?

+ Have you continuously jumped right over "like"—as in "I like you" and "Our goals, values, and ideas are alike"—right into instant gratification, cave-in-to-chemistry territory?

(If you answer "yes" to any of the above, don't worry. By the time we get to the end of the "It's *you*" chapters, you'll find ways to change those yesses into more positive "not anymores!")

Finally, go over the qualities you love in your friends and look for those in every man. This will take you out of any physical attractiveness mindset and put you right into what's important: the qualities that make for someone who makes *you* feel cared for, comfortable, and confident.

The best way to get him talking without making him feel like he's in the middle of a job interview is to have a list of questions that *sound* conversational, but are really structured so that you can say, "Oh really . . . That's interesting. Why?" It's a total police technique. Ask a question that gets 'em telling a story in which they get to be the center of attention, they will say something that gives off clues that you can use. Some good ones to incorporate:

+ What achievement are you most proud of?

+ What do you think is the most important quality you got from your parents?

+ What would be your dream job?

+ What do you most want out of a vacation?

Bonus: Think about your own answers—*bam!* You've also gained some insight on yourself.

And if he does say something that you would find undesirable in a friend? Unless it's completely heinous ("My dream job? I think being a pimp would be fun. . . ."), keep it in your brain's lockbox for future consideration. If you don't know the guy very well but he seems to have all the Non-Negotiables in place, it's possible that he could be nervous or misinterpreted. Give him some time to either trump it or trip himself up with it.

Choosing To Be Choosy

First, don't waste the work. You've put a whole lot of thought into your behaviors and needs. Always review them before a date so that these revelations are in the back of your mind.

Next, don't disregard discomfort. If there's something that your date says or does that triggers a negative response—especially an unpleasant one that feels familiar—trust your instincts. Choose to end the date and never accept another one from him.

Then, don't date just one guy at a time. Just because you both had a great time on a first date and have agreed to go on another one doesn't mean you are now a couple and you owe him some kind of loyalty or fidelity (don't forget—that goes *both* ways!). Knowing you have another date in the wings within the next day or so allows you to think clearly and be Choosy.

Finally, pay attention. Very often, a guy will say things that give off clues as to whether he's worth a second date—or if he's not in sync with your thinking that another date night is in the bag. If he's saying things that are contrary to what you sincerely believe and feel—believe him. If he's very vague about *when* he'll call you or *what* he's thinking about with respect to future plans, don't wait for the phone to ring. (If it does, great! If not, you won't beat yourself up over it.) With that in mind, guys are totally flattered and taken by a woman who stops talking about herself long enough to ask questions and encourage them to talk about themselves. Bottom line: The more you flatter, the more info you'll gather!

Once you go Choosy, you'll realize how much easier it is than the rigidity of Two Picky or the humiliation of Not Picky Enough. Now you need to extend that Choose-ability into what you decide to carry with you on the road to Dateworthiness!

Chapter 4

Good Luggage from Bad Baggage

So, what kind of traveler are you? Are you sporting an under-the-seat bag, or does the entire Samsonite line accompany you on every outing? Familiar with freight charges? Do you brag about traveling light when, in reality, you are secretly hoping that the over-packed carry-on you're wheeling won't burst and explode its contents throughout the overhead compartment?

It's pretty much a given that you will be transporting some kind of baggage with you on your relationship road trip. Unfortunately, as we leave one relationship location for the new destination, too many of us decide to keep all the souvenirs—no matter how silly or chipped they are—we've gathered during our stay. And because the bag we originally brought with us is now too full, we merely pick up another one, pack up, and go on with our slightly heavier load.

Sigh. Wouldn't it be nice to carry just the most-needed essentials and trust that you can just pick up anything you needed upon arrival?

It can happen. But first, you need to distinguish the difference between Good Luggage and Bad Baggage—what you should be packing and the stuff you should pack off to some garbage dump.

Bad Baggage

Bad Baggage has less to do with the actual bags and a whole lot to do with what you're carrying around. Trust me—serious garbage lugged around in Louis Vuitton is still serious garbage. (Or, I guess in the case of Vuitton, I should refer to it as gar-*bahj*.)

Bad Baggage is, essentially, lousy love lessons: things you learned that color your perspective about the next guy you meet before you're even an hour into the date. It's damaging habits and toxic information from love gone wrong that you've somehow convinced yourself are truths to live by. It's poisonous souvenirs of relationships past that you didn't leave behind because you figured that you paid for 'em (some dearly) and it just seemed . . . wasteful . . . to not bring them along and hope they actually turned into something useful.

> RelationTip: If you don't dump your Bad Baggage <u>before</u> you go for that next date, you will inevitably dump it <u>on</u> him.

Hate to tell you this, but just because something came with a cost, it doesn't necessarily make it valuable.

With that in mind, I want you to stop what you're doing right now (okay, not *right* now—but certainly at the end of this chapter), grab paper and pen, and write down every relationship that you feel violated your faith in love or undermined your confidence. I want you to explore:

Childhood memories. You may not have been dating, but you were certainly learning about relating. The pain and confusion of witnessing ugly interactions between parents (either between mom and dad, or a divorced parent plus significant other) can often stick to the bottom of our bags.

Teen trauma. Hormonal surges make even the shiest of teens feel the urge to put their toes into the dating pool. Unfortunately, this is the age when kids can be most cruel, and when even the smallest of slights can be seen as incredibly humiliating. If the guy you liked made fun of you or laid blows to your ego, you could still be carrying those wounds. You thought that was so yesterday . . . but oops! It surfaced again.

Dating drama. Your rat radar was wrong. Your gaydar wasn't much better. This one lied, that one broke your heart. Cheaters, and crazies, and commitment-phobes, oh *my*! In order not to make the same mistakes over again, you mistakenly store those bad experiences—and you end up with no gems in all that rough stuff.

Feel like you're writing a novel? Good—keep going. Lay it all out there, right in front of you so you can see those dating disasters come to life. I'm betting there's stuff there you haven't *actively* thought about in ages—like that fifth grade crush who crushed your heart. And I'm betting that some of it still hurts a little. Or a lot.

RelationTip: Write down what worries you—you can only edit and erase what you can clearly see.

The first thing you should do: Read through those pages and sing a verse of Destiny's Child's "I'm a Survivor." No kidding. Look at what your heart has been through, and yet you *still* picked up this book. Despite any past damage, you *still believe* that you can be—and find—a Dateworthy person.

Allow yourself a little gloat time. Go ahead. You deserve it. Then . . . back to work.

The next thing you should do is think about how each of these ugly moments hurt you and write that down next to the incident. For example: You wrote about when you caught Billy cheating with your best friend. This is a "hurt my ability to trust" issue.

Then, go over in your mind how you've allowed each hurt to continue to wound you with respect to relationships, and write that down as well. Back to our example: You wrote that Billy's cheating hurt your ability to trust. As you think about that, you might realize that your reaction to that inability to trust was to accuse the next guy of cheating or lying, even though there's nothing remotely similar between him and Billy.

Wow. Look at all that Bad Baggage. What a mess!

Now: Reread those pages. Out loud. And after every item you utter, I want you to say, "So what?"

"I caught Billy cheating on me with my best friend." So what?

"My dad never told me I was beautiful." So what?

"George admitted he only used me for sex." So what?

I know. You're thinking: "So *what*? Whaddya mean, 'So what?' It *hurt* me. It was painful. I put on like twenty chocolate pounds!"

Sorry about that (especially about those out-of-love-handles), but will hanging on to it change what happened? No. As a matter of fact, hanging on to all that Bad Baggage only allows those jerks to

Dating Diary

When I met Craig, I was just coming off a relationship with someone who had lied to me on a daily basis. I insisted on absolute honesty, and Craig told me everything. I never reacted badly to anything he revealed (even if it was a story about a girl flirting with him) to encourage the truth telling.

One night he came over right after the gym and as he showered, I found myself . . . going through his gym bag. I felt guilty. I felt so bad about my Bad Baggage behavior that he had to endure. But then I came across these pictures of a recent night out with the guys that he claimed had been so boring . . . and there were strippers in every shot. I wigged out, went into the bathroom, and flung the pictures at him. "You liar! Why didn't you mention this to me? You know I insist that even if I don't like what I'm hearing, I always want the truth!" Angry that I went through his gym bag, he finished up and left. Later, he called and said, "I'm sorry. I'm just so used to not mentioning stuff like that because my last girlfriend would actually get physical over stuff like that." Hmmm . . . Sounds like I wasn't the only one carrying Bad Baggage.

live on in your jurisdiction. Why in the world do you want to give them so much power over you?

By asking yourself, "So what?" about each of your issues, you've just taken the wind out of their heavy sails . . . at least, temporarily. Now that you've been able to loosen that tight grip on your Bad Baggage, set it down . . . and stay open to picking up some Good Luggage.

Good Luggage

Once again, we're not talking designer labels or name brands here. We're talking about the *quality* of what you choose to take with you from one relationship to the next.

Because it actually is a good thing to take some love lessons with you . . . just not Bad Baggage lousy ones. The Good Luggage love lesson is about finding the positive from past negative experiences. It's about taking what you've learned from feeling set up or hurt and using it in a practical—not prejudicial—way.

Okay. There's a good reason why I had you go over and over your Bad Baggage list. And why I'll wait til the end of this chapter to give you a final shred and burn assignment. It's because I wanted you still to have the evidence of your relating history in front of you so that we can attempt to rewrite—and rewire—what you *should* be extracting from those experiences.

You already know what kind of negative emotions you picked up from being burned and broken up with. Let's take our earlier example of Billy to illustrate how to turn the Bad Baggage into a powerfully Good Luggage moment.

Okay, so Billy cheated on you with your best friend. This was a "hurt your ability to trust" issue. The Bad Baggage you carried with that: You were quick to accuse—or at the very least, suspect—the next guy you dated of having the capability of lying and cheating as well. Then you reread, out loud, "I caught Billy cheating on me with my best friend," and followed it up with, *"So what?"* And with that, you let go of the handle of your Bad Baggage.

But I know how tempting it is to pick that handle back up . . . unless you have something better to put in its place. And that's just what we're going to do.

Dating Diary

For the longest time, I was a dating and discarding demon. After a few dates, I could totally tell which guys were whipped and which ones deserved to be, and I was pretty blasé about that. When I met Frank, I felt like I had met my male equivalent—he was outgoing, full of fun and laughter, and I totally knew that he was total relationship material. We had so much in common (including: we both thought I was fantastic), and I knew that this guy would rather cut off his right arm than ever do anything to hurt me. And then I caught that same right arm around someone else a few months later. I didn't see it coming, and I was devastated—and, for the longest time, so quick to kick every date to the curb if I found myself liking him too much. I didn't trust them because I no longer trusted my ability to pick the good guys. It took some time to realize that every date was a threesome—me, the guy, and Frank.

Enter the Positive Spin Zone

Trusting others, trusting yourself . . . these are just two of the top six sick-to-your-stomach, past-experience fears my readers most often feel. Their question: How do I *not* allow my Bad Baggage emotions to emerge when I'm feeling one of those fears? My answer: Practice substituting a Good Luggage lesson for them. Let's take a look at how you can put a positive spin on a negative situation.

1. Trusting Others

    Bad Baggage Emotion: I have lost my ability to trust and am now extremely judgmental.

Good Luggage Lesson: I know better than to put my trust in anyone too soon but am willing to give a person the opportunity to earn it.

2. Trusting Yourself

Bad Baggage Emotion: I am afraid of falling for the wrong guy again.

Good Luggage Lesson: I will date with the idea of building friendships first.

3. Desperation

Bad Baggage Emotion: I'll do what it takes to please a guy so that I won't get dumped.

Good Luggage Lesson: I'll take my time to weed out the men who just want to sleep with anybody and narrow the group down to men who wait because they are truly interested.

4. Oversensitivity

Bad Baggage Emotion: If I see one thing that brings up memories of an ex, I'm outta there.

Good Luggage Lesson: I will keep my eyes and ears open for his ideas on things that are vital (particularly those Non-Negotiables!) and judge him on standards, not comparisons.

5. Resignation

Bad Baggage Emotion: If I don't expect too much, I will not get hurt again.

Good Luggage Lesson: If I expect to get what I'm prepared to give, I won't get hurt.

6. Insecurity

Bad Baggage Emotion: I'm not pretty/thin/smart enough to be Choosy.

Dating Diary

Darren was funny, smart, and owned some kind of word-processing hardware company. After several disastrous relationships, I had developed a hard-nose reporter style of question and answer, and proceeded to go into it to make sure this guy was dating material. He answered every query with the kind of answers I really wanted to hear. And then, I said, "Too funny. It's almost like someone coached you on everything I need out of a man." He laughed and then told me that he had to call his partner. When he came back to the table, he said, "It's been great, but I really have to get back to the office. I'll call you . . ." Kiss. Hug. Parting of ways. And then . . . nothing. Yet another guy that I really wanted a second date from but who disappeared into some strange Manhattan Bermuda Triangle, never to be heard from again.

I ran into him at a club about a month later, and I confronted him. "You really want to know?" "Yes, I have to know!" I said. "Well," he replied, not looking at me, "I felt like you were interviewing me for some kind of job. Talking to you just wasn't any fun. It's like you were this robot with a list and no personality."

Ouch. Okay, "It's not you, it's me," would've stung less. But in the long run, the truth was kinder and another step toward Dateworthiness.

Lesson learned: Casual, flirty questions? Fun and flattering. Interrogation tactics? Downright scary.

Good Luggage Lesson: I deserve someone who is worth all the love, support, caring, and kindness I have to offer. (Or my favorite mantra: I may not be Catherine Zeta-Jones, but neither is she until the makeup and hair people arrive.)

Picking out the Pieces

Now that you know how to replace Bad Baggage with Good Luggage, let's talk about paring down to the essential items. Good Luggage is all about getting down to a few, well-made, well-thought-out, easy-to-carry pieces that travel well. It's about getting the type of information that's important to keeping you from being hurt without making you sound like a dating drill sergeant. It's a subtle fact-finding mission to avoid a disastrous rerun situation.

✦ RelationTip: Reduce your queries to just the essentials—if there's too much checking out, he will check out.

Packing for your Dateworthy destination is a lot like packing for any vacation: You want to take your time thinking about the items that you can count on to make you look good and that work well when they are put together. Once you make sure that they are in good condition (you never want to let them see sweat stains!), pack them the night before . . . and last minute, throw in that one flirty, colorful, fun new accessory that goes with the essentials, but which gives your look a little originality.

Got that? You're packing pieces that make you feel confident and pulled together without too much effort so that you can concentrate on the date at hand. You want to make sure that while you're practicing Good Luggage techniques, the wonderful, original fun person that is you comes shining through. Let's break it down to the essential stuff.

Have a few "stock" stories on hand that highlight your Non-

Negotiables (fun, interesting stories about guys who cheated or smoked or were uninterested in basic hygiene). Even if they're *your* personal experience, say it happened to a friend to keep the mood light. It's an easy way to let him know what you find worthy in a person, and in turn, gives him the idea that you understand your own Dateworthiness as well.

If he says something that immediately sounds a little odd or downright disconcerting to you, don't file it in the overhead compartment for a best-friend analysis later. Ask, "What do you mean by that?" in a casual, friendly way for further info. After all, it's possible you just had Bad Baggage reflux and heard the story differently than it was meant.

Be aware that lots of questions lobbed at you—and almost no information from him—could mean he's carrying some seriously banged-up Bad Baggage of his own and he's less interested than insecure. Always try to end every third answer with, "And what about you? I bet you've got some interesting stories about that!"

Carry on, but don't allow yourself to get carried away. Never—I repeat, *ever*—do any kind of alcohol on a first date, especially if it's your first time out with your Good Luggage. You cannot believe the way alcohol stains the brain and all Good Luggage lessons go down the drain!

Don't Check It—Chuck It!

Just when you though you were Bad Baggageless . . . you come across some awful accessories in a hidden compartment. Check them out before checking in, and chuck any of the following:

Shun comparisons. If he looks like your ex, sounds like your ex, walks like your ex—that's probably due to a physical typecasting thing you did. If, however, his personality is just like that awful ex, *duck!*

Leave Miss Trust—or Mz.Trust—in either extreme, at the door. Ms. Benefit of the Doubt is the best of both worlds.

Fend off fear of failure. This is not a contest—it's a date. And even if one of you gets voted off "Has Potential Island"—*so what?* There's another reality dating show right around the corner.

Skip the sexual healing. Heading straight for the sack is unsacktisfactory and the best way to do some serious damage to the Good Luggage and self-worthfullness you've worked so hard to claim. As you read on, you'll understand why just because you *can* have sex whenever you want to doesn't mean you *should*. As a matter of fact—to just say no when everyone else is saying yes makes you the ultimate challenge.

Correct selective hearing. If he says, "I change girls the way I do socks," don't assume that he's laundry-challenged and wearing the same ones for weeks on end. I can't begin to tell you how many letters I've received from ladies who write, "He *said* he doesn't know if he'll ever commit again, but it could be because he was hurt really bad by some awful woman and he just needs some time. . . ." Hear what he says. Really listen. Mull it over later. Keep it in your no-spin zone. And then, if you decide that you are both on different pages, move on.

Good Luggage from Bad Baggage—finding a positive lesson to live by instead of dwelling on the negative aspect of crappy experiences—may take a little practice. Don't put it off—deal with the Bad Baggage now before the load gets any heavier!

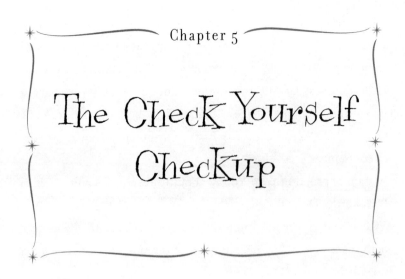

Chapter 5

The Check Yourself Checkup

Let's just be up front, right here, right now.

Despite the fact that I'm giving you a Check Yourself Checkup, I am *soooo* not judging you. Testing you? Sure. Think of it as DateMistress Dennie's dating orders to make you stay vigilant through self-examination.

After all, we've just been through a whole "It's *you*" section, which calls for some serious self-reflection and work. It was a necessary section to start out with exactly because that Get-out-of-Relationship-Free utterance, "It's not you . . . it's *me*," has often caused us to wonder if in fact, the break-up *could've* been avoided if we had practiced personal defensive dating awareness.

And let's be really straight with each other. As you went through those most-bound-to-be-broken-up-with behavior types, didn't you kind of laugh and shake your head because as you read each description, a relatable, dating disaster moment popped into your head? And when you started reading about rebounding and rerunning, didn't you actually stop a second and admit that yes, last Friday night's date fit the sitcom routine? Didn't you have a sky-opening, choir-of-angels-singing, light-bulb moment of confession that, "Yup, I guess I *have* contributed to undateworthy circumstances"?

I am *so* proud of you. You're about to receive your first belt in Dateworthy Defense.

That said, before you can really feel that you are truly able to recognize and reject "It's *you*" disorders, you must check yourself via the Check Yourself Checkup.

The checkup is comprised of two parts. First, there's a quiz to get you to think back on some of what we discussed. (That's right, a quiz—this is the one opportunity I approve of you *scoring*, if you know what I mean. . . . Oh, come on, you *know* what I mean!) Second, there's a series of lists that you should actually copy and put on your bedroom mirror. It's a good spot while dating because, hey . . . until it's a *relationship*, no one should be in your bedroom anyway. But we shall get to that in chapter 6.

Now, when you're taking the quiz, there's no flipping to the previous chapters until you are so absolutely, positively *stumped* that you have no other choice. Then it's okay—it means that you really racked your brain, and that next time, you won't forget what you worked yourself into such a frenzy to remember!

The Check Yourself Quiz

Read the following questions and circle true or false. Be Choosy—pick one answer only. Be self-worthfull—confident in your ability to know what's right. Be honest—no fair peeking! And take your time—Dateworthy, like Rome, wasn't built in a day.

T F   1. As a self-described, dating-disaster-loser-magnet, the common denominator in all your bad choices is usually circumstances that are out of your control.

T F   2. Putting your hobbies aside for his and really taking on his point of view shows an ability to compromise, which is a good dating skill to have.

T F   3. There's nothing wrong with picking a fight if it means passionate make-up sessions.

T F   4. It's important to know right off the bat what a guy's marriage potential is.

T F   5. It's never a good idea to pursue someone who doesn't immediately make you weak in the knees.

T F   6. Your list of Non-Negotiables must include honesty, education, respect, and an intense attraction.

T F   7. Technically, if you're the one who did the breaking up, you are not a rebounder.

T F   8. The best way to get past a spoiled romance is to start a fresh one with yourself.

T F   9. After a breakup, you're better off being alone with your thoughts.

T F   10. Depression is a phase that you go through only if you were dumped.

T F 11. Your Enlist to Resist ensemble is to be used only in emergencies.

T F 12. The best way to deal with the pain of rejection is head-on, as soon as possible.

T F 13. Writing out a Do Not Apply personals ad is a terrific get-a-grip project that you can do to recognize and exorcise past undateworthy guys.

T F 14. You're in rebound mode if every sentence is "ex-rated."

T F 15. There's nothing wrong with preferring a very specific physical type.

T F 16. Only men are visually stimulated.

T F 17. Being Picky is better than not being Picky at all.

T F 18. Only desperate women man plan.

T F 19. The "out of your league" mindset is a sign of insecurity.

T F 20. Fanzines, movies, and soap operas give unrealistic views of what's important in a boyfriend.

T F 21. If you've been cheated on before, you can automatically spot another cheater within the first 20 minutes of a date.

T F 22. Bad Baggage is your best defense against getting hurt.

T F 23. You can have too much Good Luggage.

T F 24. There's no value in strolling down bad memory lane.

T F 25. Dateworthiness: You're either born with it or forget it.

Answers

1. False. Being able to admit that you are the common denominator—and not chalking bad dates up to fate—gives you the power to take charge and remaster those disasters.

2. False. Becoming a boyfriend blend is being a Shadow, one of the most-bound-to-be-broken-up-with behavior types. Compromise means being able to share and/or the willingness to allow him to have something he calls his own ("Pig racing? Oh, honey, you go and have fun—I'm going shoe shopping").

3. False. There's something severely lacking in your connection if what it takes to find passion is to pick a fight.

4. False. Person potential? Yes. Whether he's just looking for a one-night booty call? Definitely. Marriage-ability? Let's put it this way: Only a few dates in is a whole lot of dates too soon.

5. False. There's nothing wrong with pursuing someone whom we find attractive, but it is absolutely wrong not to allow ourselves to give someone who is funny, smart, kind, and seemingly thoughtful a chance. One of the most recurring stories I hear from women is that the one time they didn't go for the guy who blew them away immediately, they found their amazing someone.

6. False. Education is a Negotiable—and intense attraction: See number 5! Honesty and respect are the only two must-includes here. Bonus points if you remembered "loyalty" and "contacts you regularly" as the other Non-Negotiables!

7. False. Perhaps you broke up because you finally had had enough of his bad behavior. Or because, once again, you

were bored and over it. Either way, if you're just out of a relationship, you are a rebounder, bound to be caught in yet another drama until you take the steps to figure out why you end up in undateworthy situations.

8. True. By taking time to reconnect with yourself—realizing and remembering the things that make you happy and proud and thankful—you will be refreshed and ready for a fresh start.

9. False. This is where your close friends and family can play a part in helping you get out the bad stuff that keeps revolving through your head and help you move forward. After all, grief shared is grief diminished.

10. False. You can feel depressed even if you were the dumper. The end of something that you had such high hopes for definitely has some sadness attached to it. Also, if you were the dumper only because of incredibly ugly behavior on his part . . . well, then, you may have dumped, but he left this relationship long before you did.

11. False. Your Enlist to Resist team is a terrific support system you should be able to turn to at any time—yes, in emergencies, but also to just bounce things around with.

12. True. If you don't deal with the pain and choose to push it aside rather than go through it, you can bet that it *will* turn into Bad Baggage that will weigh on you down the road.

13. True. Actually writing out a list of all the characters that need *not* apply based on exes past is a great way to get a grip on what you *should* be looking for.

14. True. If you cannot stop talking about him, you're not over him—but your date will be over you in a hurry.

15. False. Being very specific—or in a word, *Picky*—with a narrow list of physical characteristics definitely cuts out potential great dates. It's okay to be attracted to certain looks—just be sure that there's more than *one* criterion on your list.

16. False. Women are incredibly visually stimulated. Unlike men, however, we are more open to what's beautiful.

17. False. Being Picky is lonelier, but not better.

18. False. Smart, successful women always plan ahead so that they have a sense of control. Desperate women operate on a "grab it so that I'll have something to take home" mentality.

19. False. Understanding what your "league" is—that is, your strengths, things you need to work on, your comfort levels—means that you have awareness of who you are and what you deserve. Remember: "Out of your league" often means less-compatible, not overqualified, to be your boyfriend.

20. True. So please, throw out those archived *Tiger Beat*s and recent *US Weekly*s and no one gets hurt.

21. False. If you figure being newly burned equals a more accurate radar, guess again. Most likely, you're just experiencing Bad Baggage reflux—that is, dumping your cheating baggage all over this guy who may not even deserve it.

22. False. Carrying around Bad Baggage—aka lousy love lessons—means being too full to make room for great potential dates.

23. True. Surprise! Too much Good Luggage—the stuff you use to override Bad Baggage—can make you look and act high-maintenance. Keep Good Luggage to a few, well-thought-out pieces.

24. False. Sometimes taking a second look at a bad memory—and then, thinking about it with a newer, more positive spin—can take the sting out of it and leave you feeling powerful.

25. False! Dateworthy just takes some practice and experience!

So . . . did you *score big*??

20–25 correct answers: If he comes a-knockin', you are *rockin'*! While you may not be fully prepared to handle the two-headed being (Curious? Keep reading!), you will definitely be able to hold your own until you get through Parts 2 and 3!

11–19 correct answers: Be careful. Your relationship could end up a relation-*slip*! You may have the basics . . . but you're a few details short of Dateworthy behavior. It sounds to me that you did a little hop and skipping over some important points. If so, I'll make it easy for you with the Part 1 review below.

If you have less than 10 correct answers: Girl, get it straight before that important date! Remember: You need to *be* Dateworthy before you can *attract* Dateworthy. Grab a highlighter, reread . . . and retest!

Check Yourself Review Checklists

Below are lists of behaviors you have to either permanently erase—or embrace—in order to keep up the "It's *not* me!" Dateworthiness you have just attained. Read through them, out loud and proud, in front of a mirror before every date and allow them to seep into your brain and become a part of your new self-worthfull mindset.

Don't feel silly. I'll recite them with you. Let's start.

Reject Bound-To-Be-Broken-Up-With Behavior Types

First, read all of the below, then say out loud with me: "I *reject* . . ." and fill in that blank with each of the following:

+ The Time Bomb: Wanting to know where the relationship is going too soon.

+ The Shadow: Giving up your sense of self.

+ The Drama Queen: Finding fighting exciting.

+ The Diva: Treating someone as "less than."

+ The First Sighter: Believing the "love at first sight only" myth.

+ The Rescuer: Falling for men who need someone to take care of them.

+ The Other Half: Dating men lacking Non-Negotiables in order to avoid being alone.

+ The People Pleaser: Going out with your parents' dream date.

+ The Money Honey: Grubbing despite gross-out factor.

+ The Green Monster: Being overly suspicious or jealous for no reason.

Rebounds and Reruns

Now, I want you to follow up the following statements with an "Absolutely!"

+ I've done the work and know I'm not in rebound mode.

+ I have my Enlist to Resist support system in place.

+ I will watch for guys who talk about their ex constantly, seem too eager to jump into something serious, or still seem bitter or unwilling to discuss past relationships.

+ I am going out to have fun, make a new friend, and think of making a love connection as a bonus.

+ I will have a list of ten visual qualities and greenlight guys with at least three of them.

+ I will date someone completely different from my "usual" type.

Two Picky or Not Picky Enough

I have done my man planning and understand the Non-Negotiables. I should demand:

+ Honesty

+ Loyalty

+ Respect

+ Makes me feel like I'm a priority.

I will avoid Two Picky judgments, such as wanting too many Non-Essentials (good dancer, wears designer clothing). I won't expect from someone anything I am unable to offer.

And I will avoid Not Picky Enough habits. For example, having a bad date is *not* better than having none, and self-worth has to come from within, not from being wanted. I know that I have the right to be treated with respect, care, and kindness and to speak up and move on when someone is treating me less than I deserve.

$\mathcal{B}$ a d $\mathcal{L}$ u g g a g e

I have worked on my Bad Baggage emotions and replaced them with Good Luggage lessons, such as:

+ Trusting others. I replaced closed-off judgment with a willingness to give a person a chance to earn trust.

+ Trusting self. I replaced fickle-falling-for with the idea of building friendships first.

+ Desperation. I replaced "I'll make you want me now" with "I'll wait for someone who wants me too."

+ Oversensitivity. I replaced ex-comparisons with a fresh page.

+ Resignation. I replaced no expectations with expecting what I'm prepared to give back.

+ Insecurity. I replaced self-worthlessness with self-worth*full*ness.

Now, go ahead and be able to fully accept that the next time he says, "It's not you, it's *me*," he's telling the truth!

In our next section, "It's *Not* You!," we'll take a look at those guys who truly are the reason why things aren't working out . . . and give you the power to avoid them. Because, after all, while it may technically no longer be *your* behavior that is causing undateworthy moments, it is still the choices *you* make that contribute to it.

intelligent **Part 2**

open-minded responsible

funny *self-aware*

It's Not You!

trusting sexy

magnetic

self-respecting

confident

passionate

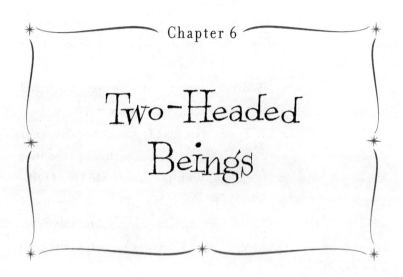

Chapter 6

Two-Headed Beings

Let's get a few things straight about this "It's *Not* You" part.

Yes, at this point, you've stamped out those seriously most-bound-to-be-broken-up-with behaviors, recognized and rejected rebounds and reruns, picked away at that old Two Picky–Not Picky Enough pattern, and gone through your Bad Baggage to glean Good Luggage materials to find your most Dateworthy inner self—heck, you even took a test to prove just how *not* you it is the next time a date goes into the Dumpster!

However . . . until you get to the end of Part 2, you technically still have some "It's *you*" responsibility, as in "It *is* you" because this is the guy *you* chose!

You can be as self-worthfull as you want to be, but it's a fact that all the insights women gain about themselves are not really enough when it comes to choosing the right guy. Men view relationships differently than women—they don't make them a priority the way we do, and they certainly approach them with a whole lot less fantasy.

Remember when we were younger and with every boyfriend we were scribbling our first names in front of their last names in big hearts that said 2GETHER 4EVER? If you looked over your boyfriend's way, he was doodling his passion, too . . . the Iron Maiden or Mötley Crüe logo, with the words METAL FOREVER! larger than life beneath. Okay, at least most of the ones I liked did. There was that one guy, Mickey, who used to draw flowers with my name in them . . . and I think he's a florist now with a boyfriend . . .

Anyway, the point is: To understand whom you are dealing with, you are going to have to start thinking like them. To get that men are different creatures . . . that some of the bad ones are really good at looking like the good guy, using dirty tricks and smooth moves based on their knowledge of our desire for relationships. ("Oh, yes, I've always wanted to be in a committed, long-term relationship with someone, but it's been so hard to find the time between volunteering at the children's burn center—I just love kids!—and being the primary family caretaker. It's been tough. With you, however, I just know I'd find quality together time. . . ." How's *that* for a fur-ball-retching moment?)

So, let's begin our guy-ology class and study what it is that makes them so different—to dissect, discover, and do away with being dude-duped. Then, once we've gotten a he-handle, we'll take a look at the dating rules you shouldn't be without.

Ready to start?

Dissecting the Two-Headed Being

Go ahead. Ask any woman about that old saying, "Two heads are better than one," as it relates to men.

She'll probably shudder or smirk or say, "When pigs fly." But I can guarantee you that she will never, *ever* come back at you with a high five, and a "Heck, yeah!"

Why?

Because she knows only one of those heads is Gray Matter Headquarters, where thought is actually processed. It's where the Non-Negotiables live and are actually put into play. And—dare I suggest it?—where communication can actually be transmitted.

And the other, smaller head (which one should *never* refer to as "smaller")? That, essentially, is merely Reaction Central, the processing area that receives orders from HQ.

And that, unfortunately, when it comes to women, Reaction Central often misinterprets the information it receives from above, turning almost any association with females into anticipation of a full-on contact sporting event.

And so goes the knowledge that is passed on from mother to daughter: "Men may have two heads; unfortunately, they only listen to the little one!"

My response? Yes, men are strongly motivated by the head that they secretly name and measure (trust me on this one—I get letters!). As a matter of fact, immediately after a guy envisions you as the mother of his children, he is picturing you doing things to him that would make *his* mother wish she had thrown out those magazines she found under his mattress.

Just because he's wired this way, however, doesn't mean that you

Dating Diary

I really wanted to go to the senior prom when I was a sophomore, but I couldn't figure out how to get someone to ask me. When I found out that Steven—a semi-popular senior—did not have a date yet, I racked my brain to figure out how to get him to take me. Then, I remembered something my mom had told me:

"Always remember that guys only want one thing. . . ."

So, with that in mind, I had a friend pull him over in the hallway to tell him that I wanted to go to the prom with him. Apparently, he wasn't all that interested till she said what I had her rehearse:

"Just be careful about letting her have any kind of chocolate—chocolate makes her really, really horny. Don't tell her I told you, though."

He asked me that afternoon.

When he came to pick me up, he was the perfect gentleman: meeting my parents, posing for pictures while he gave me my wrist corsage. When we got to the car, he said, "I have another present for you," and

don't have the power to reroute most of that electricity into something more in current with your new sense of self-worthfullness.

Log this into your frontal lobe: Reaction Central is merely the cheering section, and without Gray Matter Headquarters' input, it's got no brain—or game—on its own. So, essentially, what *you* choose to feed into Gray Matter HQ has everything to do with bringing out the worthy in your date.

Are you surprised that you actually have that kind of power?

handed me a wrapped package. I opened it to find a giant Hershey's bar and a package of Stella D'Oro Swiss Fudge cookies.

"Thanks so much—I'll eat these later so that I don't ruin my appetite!"

Steven glanced over at me while driving and said, "Oh, that's okay. I'm sure you can have a few now. As a matter of fact, why don't we share some?"

I unwrapped the Hershey bar, broke off a piece and put it in his mouth. Then promptly closed it up. "Nope. Later!"

After the prom, Steven drove me home and brought up the chocolate again. When he pulled over and parked a few houses from my parents' driveway, I opened up the cookies and had a few ooohing and aaahing moments over how good they were. Then I gathered up the rest of the chocolate and opened the door.

"Thanks so much for the night out and the chocolate. You are such a nice guy!" I got out and walked up my driveway. Man, I thought. That was too easy.

Girl, you just copped to and conquered a whole bunch of most-bound-to-be-broken-up-with behavior types. Of *course* you can control your dating destiny!

But just as you needed to gain insight into your undateworthy behaviors in order to conquer them, you're now going to have to get into a guy's head—that is, Gray Matter HQ—to understand how to get your information routed correctly through the "male room."

RelationTip: Guys won't ask for directions once they are in the driver's seat, so never let him take the wheel before he knows exactly where _you_ want to go.

Sex, Lies, and Whys

Let's get right to the basics. There's nothing deep about a dude's dating doctrine. Actually, when it comes to relationships, his brain breaks down into five easy pieces.

1. Men Love Sex

I know. Plenty of women love sex, too. But men, by and far, can enjoy sex without having any kind of emotional ties to it.

I know. Calm down. Plenty of women can have sex-as-sport, as well. And _Cosmopolitan_—the Holy Grail of the fabulous, female single—has not only helped us learn how to get it when we want it; it has taken the guilt out of the pleasure.

The difference is that somewhere in between the meaningless sack-hopping, women stop long enough to take the relationship quiz.

Men don't buy dating books. Or check out dating horoscopes. Or really read articles that don't just pertain to solo interests. Because they know that women do. And they learn pretty quickly that women will communicate to them exactly what it takes to be the kind of guy they could fall for. (With any luck, fall-into-bed for.) They will act accordingly, say all the right things, and even the most honest will lie if it means they can have a sexual encounter.

Now, before you throw your hands up and consider collecting those QVC dolls, reread the above paragraph. Notice something?

That's right. I just told you that men *can* actually listen. And they *do* if it means they may get that much closer to winning what they want.

That said, it's important to lay the groundwork of the dating game you are willing to play so that he understands that he's got work ahead of him—and so that if he's really not interested, he doesn't waste your time and his. Also important: Do not change those rules as you go along, or he'll feel that he can do the same. (More on these rules starting on page 90.)

2. Men Are Visual

Yes, I know, women certainly can appreciate the Depp facial factor, but . . . sorry, ladies, the men win hands down on this one. (And if that's not true in your case? Get thee back to Part 1!)

Case in point: Troll-like, powerful, rich men want the pinup queens. Pinups get past the troll-like looks because the power and wealth turn 'em on. And another nail in the visual coffin: Way more porn Web sites cater to men than women.

But hold on.

RelationTip: A woman often will overlook a guy's looks if he makes her feel incredibly beautiful.

While some men are incredibly superficial, most do not require you to be a beauty queen to get their attention. The good news about the visual part is that men can appreciate *all* types of variations on the female form. Yes, men may look at *Playboy*, but that doesn't mean that they also don't have their own very individual turn-ons that cause them to check—and then ask—you out. Trust me on this: I've found plenty of small-breasts-big-butt-thick-calves-loving guys out there.

With that in mind, you have to remember that when you dress to accentuate your positives on a date, Gray Matter Headquarters is shooting images fast and furiously to Reaction Central without any kind of mental processing. That is why, once again, the sooner you lay out your dating rules, the more likely you'll be able to get Gray Matter HQ to reign in Reaction Central.

3. Men Believe in Fairy Tales

Women do, too . . . but just not in the same way.

Snow White. Cinderella. Sleeping Beauty. Rapunzel. Their stories all had one thing in common: After they all caught their prince's interest, none of them was exactly easy to hook up with.

That's right. What little boys come away with is that the girl worth going after is the girl who makes them prove what they are made of. Guys really like a challenge. Not an impossible-odds, unsure-there's-payoff-potential challenge—but certainly one that keeps them interested.

While presenting a challenge to a man—particularly one that has to do with sexual standards—in no way guarantees he'll stick around and become a significant other, it *does* have certain merits:

+ There's an immediate weeding out of the One Night Standers;

+ If he does like you, it gives him more time to see you as a person, and not just a sexual object; and

+ It gives you more time to see if he's worth becoming intimate with.

And don't forget: A challenge isn't always sexual. Having your own opinions that are contrary to his and not always being available

Dating Diary

When I saw Ed's personal ad, I was absolutely sure he had written it with me in mind. "Looking for a woman who is smart, funny, and is in love with the way love happens in the old black-and-white movies." Dog and chocolate-chip-cookie lover. Appreciated the lost art of kissing. He said he resembled Tom Cruise. I responded immediately.

Despite the fact that the only resemblance he had to Tom was in the height department, our first date was wonderfully romantic and lots of fun. He surprised me on the second date with my favorite flowers (tulips), favorite restaurant, and most-loved tunes on the car stereo. Wow, I thought—a guy who not only really listens but cares enough to deliver.

As we pulled up to my apartment, he pulled me in for what I thought was an innocent make-out session. I even allowed him to be a little more intimate because I felt so happy and trusting and sure that he'd remember something else that I told him: I didn't believe in sex in the first two months of dating let alone on the first date.

In a minute, that mixed signal proved to be the beginning of a fight to get his hands off me. I kept saying, "Stop." He kept pushing. I decided it was time to go. Then he got mad and said, "Oh come on . . . I gave you everything, now it's your turn to make me happy." In one frightening moment, he roughly grabbed my bra at the front and tried to shove a hand down my jeans. I reached behind me and opened the door, and just as we both discovered that I was wearing a front-clip bra that evening, I fell right out of the car. There were enough people around for him to decide not to cause a further scene, and he said nothing when I screamed "Asshole!" and slammed the door.

Dating Diary

I was at a used car lot, keeping my sister company. As she was haggling for a car, this very black, very shiny Monte Carlo pulled up to the lot of-fice . . . and out came all 6'3" of Jazz. He was gorgeous in that '80s Tom Selleck way, and when he stopped and stared at me, I flashed him my most fabulous smile. And then I noticed there was a girl in the passenger seat.

I made a face and turned away, which froze him for about a second, and then he continued across the lot to say hello. We looked each other over, and then I told him that I wasn't interested in talking to a guy with a girlfriend. He said it wasn't a girlfriend—just a friend that was a girl—and asked if I'd consider giving him my number. I said no and turned away. He headed back to his original destination—the lot office—and then left. Later he called me.

"How did you get my number?" I asked. "From Craig at the car place—I gave him five bucks for it." I said, "Sorry, but still not interested in a guy with a girlfriend." Before I could hang up, he said, "Please, if you don't

for dates because you are legitimately—and honestly—dating others . . . total challenge shake-up.

4. Men Will Forego Sex for Ego Attention

If you want to make a man feel good without compromising on your dating standards, then reach out and stroke . . . that ego.

No kidding. I'll never forget speaking to a male psychologist

believe me, call Craig—I'm telling you, I'm single." I hung up. He
called . . . and then Craig called . . . consistently for the next few days until
I gave him a chance. And I did. And when I became the girlfriend, he
cheated on me with the next challenge.

On the flip side:

Tim was one of the nicest, most giving guys ever to be built like a yield
sign. Everything he did was . . . so nice. So I constantly picked fights
about ridiculous things just to see what he looked like with a little fire
in his eyes—you know, the way guys were in the girl-meets-boy, boy-
loses-girl, girl-and-boy-get-back-together-after-passionate-disagreement
movies. Know what? At first, it was thrilling to constantly have make-up
make-out sessions. And I think he at first thought it was fun to have to
rack his brain to try to win me back. And then . . . boy not only got rid of
girl, but he definitely didn't have the energy to think about getting back
together.

friend years and years ago who told me that guys invest their egos
in two places: the bedroom and the boardroom. So I asked him,
"What do you do if you really don't know him in either ca-
pacity?" He said, "Compliment his physical and mental attributes
so that he *thinks* you believe that he's dynamic in both areas
anyway."

I tested the theory. I told Freddy what gorgeous shoulders and
arms he had. I constantly asked Charlie about his day at work, and

if he discussed a decision he made, I would say, "I am so impressed with the way you handled that."

Ladies . . . that advice was golden. I not only saw the light of confidence glow in their eyes, but I also noticed a serious upswing in second dates.

RelationTip: Someone who feels respected respects your feelings in return.

5. Men Do Want Relationships

Sex without strings may be king, but deep down, men really do hope that they can meet someone. . . . Okay, yes, someone to have regular sex with, but also someone who can make them feel loved, needed . . . important. No kidding.

Don't cue the romantic music just yet: Just because he wants a relationship doesn't mean he puts finding one in his top-priority file. Which means that setting the tone, pace, and direction of the dating game is strictly going to be up to the person who has already worked to put Dateworthiness first—you. That means being upfront about how you expect to be treated, and taking your time to really get to know his motives and what he's really made of. (And then, when the time is right, leading the conversation into exclusive territory . . . but we've still got to get through a few dates before we even reach that relationship plateau.)

Trailer Talk

Remember what I said about tone, pace, and direction?

Well, you know what he wants: to play the sexually fulfilled leading man. It's up to you, however, to direct this dating picture, and you can only do that by letting him know right off the bat that you're looking for the nice-guy-that-earns-the-girl type.

And you're going to do it by giving him a little bit of story line . . . via what I call Trailer Talk.

Think about it: What makes you excited about going out to see a new flick? The movie trailer, of course.

The trailer is a quick, edited preview of movie highlights that gives you the basic idea of what the film is all about yet still leaves you anticipating where the story will take you. It also provides a rating—important to know ahead of time so that you can make an informed choice between bringing your ultra-conservative mom or your anything-goes girlfriend.

The first-date Trailer Talk works in a similar way.

Good Trailer Talk provides the information you want a guy to know in a format that won't lose his attention (that is, quick and to the point so that Gray Matter Headquarters can get back to sending visuals to Reaction Central). It should be delivered in a tone that's lighthearted yet matter-of-fact (guys prefer action and comedy over serious story lines weighed down with heavy symbolism); then it should end quickly so that you can move on to more fun date activities—like flirting and the dessert menu. It's talking to men the way men do: simple, direct, and without any of that female "I hope he reads between the lines" stuff.

Now let's do the math: If you take the two-headed being basics, divide it by your dating rules, and then add your trailer talk, what do you get?

Why, Gray Matter Guy'd-lines, of course!

Fundamentally, this is a guideline of lines you can give to guys to combat their five-easy-pieces thought process. I've made it easy for you by setting up each of his wants—like sex—and guiding you through what to say to keep him in check—and wanting to check you out on later dates.

Gray Matter Guy'd-line #1: Men like sex.

Your rule should be: No sex on the first date. (Actually, I'd like to see you substitute first date with "first few dates," but that's purely a personal choice.)

Your line should be: "It may sound old-fashioned, but I make it a rule that I never have sex on the first date."

Gray Matter Guy'd-line #2: Men are visual.

Your rule should be: Don't bring sex—and sexual images—into conversation.

Your line should be: "You know what? Instead of sex, let's talk more about something else. Tell me about what you do for a living."

Gray Matter Guy'd-line #3: Men believe in fairy tales.

Your rule should be: Never change the rules to lessen the challenge.

Your line should be: "I think the more a guy and girl get to know each other, the more amazing it is when they finally get together."

Gray Matter Guy'd-line #4: Men will forego sex for ego attention.

Your rule should be: Compliment without sexual innuendo.

Your line should be: "You're definitely one of the smartest guys I've met. What's your opinion on [a topic you can actually discuss]?" Or: "You have the nicest eyes/smile. Do you take after your mom or dad?" (Nothing knocks out Reaction Central like parent chat.)

Gray Matter Guy'd-line #5: Men do want relationships (it's just not as much a priority as sex!).

Your rule should be: Make getting to know the person—not relationship potential *or* sex—the priority on a first date.

Your line should be: "How about we leave all that intimate stuff out of this conversation and save it for when we need something to talk about a few dates from now?" (How's that for a challenge?)

Disclaimer time: While I can guarantee that Gray Matter Headquarters will be in charge during the date if you produce a very tight trailer to capture his attention, I cannot promise you what he'll send to Reaction Central later when he stops thinking about your words and starts picturing what you were wearing underneath that not-so-provocative outfit.

Alrighty, then. You've hit up Gray Matter Headquarters with something that will need some serious processing. If this guy is a total, undateworthy player, you won't hear from him again. And if he's just your average two-headed being with Dateworthy potential, I promise you he'll at least be second-date-curious.

And speaking of Dateworthiness—let's take a look at my version of the "spaghetti western". . . .

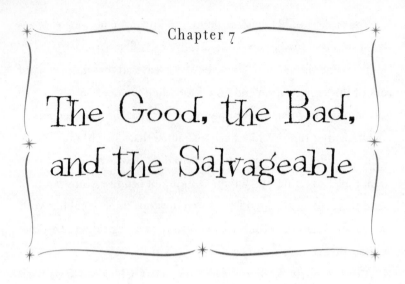

Chapter 7

The Good, the Bad, and the Salvageable

I hear it all the time.

"All the good ones are taken."

And to that I respond with a slap and a heartfelt, "Snap out of it already!"

Okay. Maybe I restrain from the physical stuff.

But I'm not kidding about snapping out of that Little Orphan Annie "Hard Knock Life" routine.

At this point, you've read some of my disastrous dating stories, so you *know* that I *totally* agree that there's a whole lot less Mr. Right-for-Yous than Mr. Right-If-You're-a-Barn-Animal types of guys. But that doesn't mean that they aren't out there. They are. And excuse me for being a little blunt, but I'm betting that you probably have already connected with one or two really good ones that you either a) bypassed, b) lost, or c) let go of because . . . well, you yourself weren't exactly in full Dateworthy bloom at the time.

But that was then. Now that you're in such incredibly Dateworthy shape, you are ready to get back out there and do what I did: Dispel the "There are no good ones left" myth.

And you know how you're going to do it?

You're going to approach this task by tapping into the DNA every woman is born with—that is, the shopping gene.

RelationTip: You can't find gold using a scrap metal Geiger counter.

Unearthing your Dateworthiness truly is a lot like shopping at one of those luxury brand outlet places. Think about it. You go to the outlet because you know that they carry well-made, designer labels. And sure enough, when you get there, the place is loaded with Calvins and Ralphs. But as you whip through the items, you realize that you have to slow down and pick through carefully because the good designer items are stuck betwixt and between some strange, cheaply made, seriously ugly unwearables. Or worse, they're only available in a size you haven't fit into since high school—and even then, it wasn't all that comfortable.

But you're fine with that, because experience has taught you to allot yourself a good amount of time so that you could move through the clothing slowly and not have to make rushed, snap decisions. And then . . . your patience and determination is rewarded. You find the perfect Ralph Lauren blouse and then a very nice pair of his dress pants in your size, but wait . . . the zipper is broken. You think: "Totally salvageable—I could fix this myself." (Or, if you're like me, you think, "Totally salvageable—

that tailor guy down the street will do it for like five bucks.")

See where I'm going here?

Dateworthy: a good perfect fit. Undateworthy: a bad style for you. And the fine line between Dateworthy and Undateworthy? Salvageable—could be good with minor adjustments, but if it needs a major overhaul, it's a bad choice. Now you just need to be an educated consumer to know the difference.

School is now in session!

The Good

Aaah, the good guy.

Of course, being Dateworthy yourself, you already know that he's got good possibilities if he's displaying Non-Negotiably correct behaviors (you know those by heart, don't you?).

But then again, despite being Dateworthy and knowing what to look for, isn't it just possible—because, as we learned in our last chapter, they *are* two-headed beings willing to do anything for sex—that he's putting up a *front*? That he's actually a baaaad sheep in good clothing?

Gold star!

You've just come upon the one good-guy black hole known as the Best Behavior Zone.

The Best Behavior Zone is that first three to four months when everyone is on his/her very best behavior—she in an effort to slip into his heart, he in an effort to have her slip into something more comfortable. Essentially, you're both putting out your greatest hits—the tried and true "best of" moments that have wowed the general dating audience before.

Dating Diary

Peter and I had only gone out a few times, and it was pretty obvious to me that he was a really good guy—and that he liked me a lot. When I had to go out of town for a few days, I asked him if he'd keep my two canaries until I got back, and he wholeheartedly said yes. I never liked those birds—they were a gift from another amorous suitor. When I got back, I screened his calls or made up excuses why I couldn't come by for the birds that day. He finally had enough: "Dennie, I did you a favor, and you're not being fair. I need you to pick up these birds today so that I can get away for the weekend. I'll see you after work tomorrow." Click.

Unfortunately, the next morning, I woke up with the start of a migraine headache that only got worse as the day progressed, and by 4:00 P.M., I knew I had to go home. I called Peter and told him why I wouldn't make it over. "Oh, no way!" he said. "You just wait in the cab, and I'll come downstairs and give them to you on your way home." Reluctantly, I agreed. When we pulled up, there was Peter, standing on the corner holding these wildly flapping birds in a very girly scroll-work cage. He bent in to give me the birds . . . and then when he saw how bad I looked, he hesitated . . . and jumped in the cab with me. He not only helped me lie down and applied a cool washcloth to my head, he ran out to find headache medicine and came back with at least four different brands. And then he slept on the couch—several inches too short for his long legs—to be nearby in case I woke up and needed anything.

Hang on. I never said that finding that one good hit single was going to be easy. But, just like when you were outlet shopping, getting that good deal—maybe even the deal of a lifetime—is absolutely possible if you keep these two Guy'd-lines in mind:

1. Time is on your side. Due to the Best Behavior Zone, even the worst of the bad guys can, at first, seem like a really good catch. Knowing that, you need to think of your dating process less as a one-night variety show and more in terms of a reality-survivor show series. That is, you allow the process to run long enough so that most of the truly bad ones (who *only* want to pull a hit-it-now-and-run maneuver) vote themselves off your island, leaving a better quality of guy for *you* to eventually eliminate.

2. You can bring more than one item into the dressing room. That's right. I'm talking about increasing your chances of finding the good ones by dating more than one seemingly Dateworthy guy at a time. (Incidentally, thinking of dating as a numbers game is a total guy behavior.) You know how you are well aware of your own Dateworthiness? Well, Dateworthy guys know it, too. Here's an interesting note: Unlike women—and because of what women say—they *realize* that they are a hot commodity and are willing to keep dating and hold out for someone just as Dateworthy as themselves. Quantity not only ups your chances of quality, but because you are so busy and unavailable, your "what a challenge" stock will rise considerably!

See a pattern here?

Good guys *allow* themselves to feel confident in their Dateworthiness—they revel in the fact that they are worth the wait and the work. Now, that's a lesson that you (and every female) would be smart to take to heart (and a concept that we will explore in the next few pages).

Now . . . let's get a good idea of what the bad ones are all about.

The Bad

Bad guys are kind of like serial killers.

They don't *look* threatening. Heck, some of the most notorious were reported to be charming. Even *handsome*. And very often, in their lives outside of the dating and relationship realm, bad guys are often good people.

But know what's the scariest thing about a bad guy?

He starts off so good, we find it incredibly hard to believe he wasn't truly that way all along. And, yes, we do this ladies—when he *does* start to show his true colors, we wonder what *we* did wrong to *make* him change.

RelationTip: The bad guys desire a woman whose main desire is the desire of a guy.

Despite all of our Dateworthy work, we still wonder if perhaps we weren't so worthy after all. Actually, because we are now so much more aware of things like the most-bound-to-be-broken-up-with behavior types, it makes our fears even worse. Why do we do this to ourselves despite knowing deep down that we are, indeed, Dateworthy?

It's that old double-standard, fostered by the culture and society we live in.

Guys don't apologize for their behavior. Girls, however, are taught from an early age to be nice, don't hurt, try to understand, apologize often, brush off compliments as nothing, never be cocky. Heck. I think that whoever made up the word "cocky" made sure it was so embarrassingly masculine that *no* woman would ever attempt to be take on that characteristic.

And you know what? The bad ones know that we are taught this way, and they take advantage of how much we want to please.

It's time to put a stop to that kind of "good girls don't" mindset right now, girlfriends.

All through this book I've stressed that you need to take responsibility for your own actions. And you believed. And you worked. And you're now worthy of better. So now, I want you to trust me on this: Good guys with expiration dates were never, ever good guys at all.

Actually, great Dateworthy guys get better with time. And now's when you need to rely on all that work you did to *become* Dateworthy and the skills you learned for self-worthfullness in order to *choose* Dateworthy men.

Are you as pumped up as I am right now?

RelationTip: You are not responsible for another's bad behavior—only for the way you choose to react to it.

Scary Signposts

Let's pretend that we are now approaching the Best Behavior Zone limits, and we're just beginning to see the following scary signposts ahead. Are you with me? Now, after you read each one of those scary signpost descriptions, let me get a "Hell no, he's *got* to go!"

Scary signpost #1: Lies. I'm not talking about finding out that

Dating Diary

Gary was my bus crush. Giant blue eyes, a great body, and man, what a smile. Eventually, what I got to know about him—he lived at home to help his mom take care of his mentally retarded sister; he was studying to be a vet—really convinced me that he was definitely a good one. So when I landed tickets to the Bruce Springsteen concert—the hottest ticket in town—I decided to ask him—the hottest ticket in town—to go with me. He said yes (turns out he was a major fan) and said that while he would like to pick me up, his schedule would only allow him to meet me there. Meet we did. And he proceeded not only to get drunk, but he started hitting on this amazing-looking girl (I'm talking, like, Victoria's Secret status here) who was in the row right in front of us. When she asked about me, he said, "Nah, she's nobody. I just wanted to go to the concert and she had tickets."

He may have been making passes at her, but I had the backstage passes on me. I told him I was going to the bathroom and never came back. And I thought . . . Don'tyoudarecryDennieDon'tyouDARE.

he may have exaggerated a bit about his fantastic skyline view (technically, if you stick your head waaaaay out the window and crank it waaaaay over to the right and put just the right strain on it, you *can* see it between two buildings). I'm talking full-blown, look-you-in-the-eye, detailed whoppers to make himself look better or more important, or provide him with excuses why things don't go his way. Remember, without trust, there is zero chance for a relationship to ever work.

Scary signpost #2: Cheating. It's too early for him to be cheating on you (you've just started dating, after all, and neither one of you *should* be committing to each other this early). But he *can* be cheating on someone *else*—with you as his unwitting scarlet woman. Don't flatter yourself into thinking that he's with you because you're the better woman. Actually, you're the better *person*—and better off, if you dump him immediately. Know this: If he cheated on her, he'll cheat on you.

Scary signpost #3: Neglect. Everyone gets busy, and sometimes, it's really hard to schedule time with someone you care about. But if this guy went from phoning all the time to never returning your phone calls—and when you do talk, he makes you feel like you're selfish for wanting him to fit you into his super-busy schedule—it's time to take him off *your* speed dial. A guy who truly cares about a girl *always* finds a way to get in touch or finds times to get together. Bottom line: If his actions make you feel like a bother, *don't bother.*

Scary signpost #4: Abuse. I know that you know that there is never, *ever* any reason for someone to physically assault you and that the only one allowed to say, "You drove me to it," is *you*—the moment the cops take him away. Abuse, however, is more than just physical; it's being criticized and put down to the point where your self-esteem crumbles. When you feel that his tearing you down is then used to build himself up (he tells you that he's used to dating much thinner women), you're being abused. Don't allow him to make you feel like you're lucky to have him. No man worth having makes you question your worth.

Scary signpost #5: Addiction. He's addicted to baseball or keeping the news channel on practically 24/7? Annoying, yes, but not scary. However, if he's addicted to drugs, alcohol, or gambling, you should absolutely move on immediately. It's imperative to keep in mind that you have to be more invested in yourself and your future than in someone who has so little investment in himself that he hasn't tried to get help. I know that a lot of people are going to try to make you—and me—feel guilty about this, but don't (I won't). Take it from someone who's been there: You don't want a man who can only manage Dateworthy on a "when I'm not incapacitated" basis.

RelationTip: Scary signposts are unisex. If you are guilty of those behaviors, you deserve a good kick to the curb until you get your act together.

Whew! Now let's recap:

You know there are good ones out there and how to go about attracting them. You get the idea of how the bad ones suck the life out of you and what to watch out for after the Best Behavior Zone ends. Now let's discuss the type of guy you'll probably find most often.

The Salvageable

Just when you think you have a handle on this good and bad thing . . . I throw in the hidden variable: the salvageable guy.

Salvageable Guy is someone who meets the Non-Negotiables, but sometimes exhibits some serious loser tendencies. He's the guy who does everything right in the Best Behavior Zone, but then one day just screws up royally.

Remember back to bad guy scary signposts and how any of that kind of behavior gives you grounds to say, "Go away"? Salvageable

Guy comes with his own set of cautionary clues—borderline behavior stuff that may turn you off, but which need to be weighed and considered with his a) Non-Negotiable consistency and b) willingness to make some concessions if it means being with you.

Bottom line: If the Non-Negotiables *aren't* consistent, and there isn't a willingness to work with you, then Salvageable Guy is just a disguise for an undateable (if not completely bad) guy whom you need to step away from so that you don't get hurt.

Cautionary Clues

Here's a checklist of Mr. Salvageables to ponder:

Cautionary clue #1: Mr. Insecurity. It's normal to feel a little insecure when you first start dating someone—especially if you really like the person and want to make a good first impression. You can tell when a guy is a little insecure because it breeds a lot of make-me-feel-like-a-great-date questions ("Are you having a good time?" "Did you like the restaurant?" "Did I ask you if you're having a good time?"). However, if he's still asking a million affirmation questions several dates in, to the point where you want to scream, "I'd have a better time if you'd just stop asking me if I am!" what's fair is to make him aware. Say, "I think it's nice that you're so concerned, but I wish you didn't need to ask me over and over again. Please relax and trust that I wouldn't be seeing you if I didn't enjoy every moment with you." If *that* doesn't stop the endless questions, answer "Want to go out?" with, "No, thanks."

Cautionary clue #2: Mr. Innuendo. It's to be expected that the more you date, the more Reaction Central starts to overtake Gray Matter Headquarters—even the good ones have a hard time holding off on that sexual healing feeling. Sexy "When will we?"

Dating Diary

I'd seen Steve for weeks at the downtown basketball courts, and I'd stand by the fence for what seemed like forever, watching the sweat drip off this perfectly tanned and toned body and from his black, curly, moppy hair. I finally decided to take matters into my own hands. The next time I showed up, I grabbed a bottle of Gatorade and used that to make my way onto the courts when he took a break and introduce myself.

We went out a few times, and then he asked me to come over just to hang out. When we got there, the place was dimly lit—mood lighting, I thought. We made out like rabid teenagers on his futon, and I kicked off my sandals. When he stopped to run to the bathroom, I realized I had lost my earring and hopped off the couch to switch on the overhead light. I stepped on something. As I turned on the light, I realized it was . . . toe nail clippings. I didn't know what was worse: those, or the roaches on the ceiling. Yup, I thought. That was mood lighting alright—without it, there was no mood at all!

When he came back and saw the picture I was seeing, he was mortified. And, being a total neat and clean freak, I freaked out and left, intent on never seeing him again. After a few weeks of dodging his calls, I finally returned one and decided that his explanation about a sloppy houseguest, coupled with how nice (and gorgeous) he was, definitely deserved a second look. We ended up dating a few more months, and yes he cleaned up his act. I'm so glad I decided that he was salvageable!

teasing, on occasion, is okay after several dates. Constant badgering, however—especially if you've made it clear that you're not ready yet—is inappropriate. If you've already been intimate and now *all* he talks about is "getting outta here and getting busy," it's time for you to let him know that as much as he thinks he's making you feel desirable, it's having the opposite effect. Because you have to deal with two heads here, the blunter the better: "It's obvious we both find each other incredibly sexy—why don't we try to see if we have more in common than that?" If this doesn't dampen his enthusiasm for finding a way to turn every topic sexual ("Wait . . . I was just talking about volunteering at church . . . how did we end up on *this* subject again?"), you need to consider that perhaps this guy really doesn't have much to offer beyond the bedroom. Communication is hard enough for men. Why pick one who will make it tougher?

Cautionary clue #3: Mr. Ego. You already know that next to sex, two-headed beings love to have their ego stroked. And actually, if he's been a good guy who treats you well, there's no reason why you shouldn't offer up regular compliments and even allow him to brag a little about some of the things he's most proud of. But, if after a while the only question he's asking you is, "Enough about me. What do *you* think of me?" then it's time for you to give him a wake-up call. Now's the time to work yourself back into the conversation. Say, "You know, I love hearing about what you're up to but sometimes I wish you would ask me about how my day was. I'm hoping that it's not because I'm boring to you, because if so, then maybe we shouldn't be dating!" Be prepared that he may need a few interjections from you at first to get him into the habit ("Do you want to hear what happened to me today?"), but that nudge is all it should take. If he remains wrapped up in his own world, rocket outta there.

Cautionary clue #4: Mr. One-Liner. It's great when you find a guy who can make you laugh—someone who always seems to come up with a quick quip or finds the funny in every situation. But if all this guy feeds you is a steady diet of one-liners for everything and *anything* ("Your kitchen burned down? Guess it's a bad time to ask for a home-cooked meal!"), that's a serious issue that needs to be addressed. Say, "You know, when you constantly turn everything I tell you into a joke, it makes me feel like you're less interested in how I'm feeling and more interested in just getting past a subject." If he responds with something funny, don't laugh. Make him squirm and see that you're serious. If that doesn't change his stand-up ways, stand *him* up.

WARNING: The following cautionary clue is one that needs immediate assessment.

Cautionary clue #5: Mr. Jealousy. It's kind of flattering, at first, to have someone like you so much he keeps trying to convince you that you don't need to be playing the dating numbers game. A little jealousy is normal at the beginning of a dating relationship, and it's okay when what it inspires is for him to be challenged to work harder at doing all the right things to win your heart. Jealousy is a problem, however, when he not only becomes overly possessive, but he tries to make you feel like you're not smart enough to watch out for player-sex-maniacs and you need to do as he says to stay safe. If his jealousy is making you uncomfortable, immediately say so: "I don't know if you realize this, but when you tell me what to do/who not to see/what not to wear, I don't like it. If you're going to act this way before we even get to a place where we would talk about commitment, then I don't want to see you anymore." The *only* Salvageable response is an apology and a complete change of attitude—any anger, hostility, or arguments about how you are *wrong* about your feelings, and you end it then and there.

And there you have it:

The good.

The bad.

The salvageable.

And the Dateworthy secret to knowing the difference: Don't get attached too early so that you can honestly evaluate which category he falls into.

Next—let's tackle the communication situation. Or, as women like to say, the lack of it!

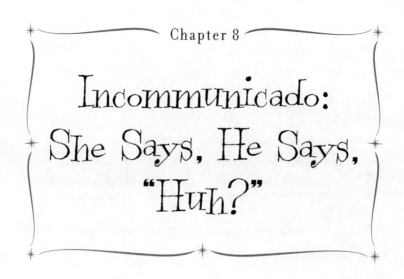

Chapter 8

Incommunicado: She Says, He Says, "Huh?"

Listen up: Men don't. (Listen up, I mean.)

And unless it's about a topic near and dear to their hearts, they don't talk much either.

Sure, they can *hear* and *respond*—they just do it in a more selective, I'm-not-initiating kind of way that is absolutely foreign and frustrating to females.

And ladies, along with a couple of other great truths in life that we absolutely, positively do not want to believe (you know, like buying a pair of pants in the size you *intend* to be will *never* be worn but will hang in your closet and taunt you), this is one you must embrace: Men will never, *ever* have the girlfriend gift of gab.

Blame it on evolution.

Back in the caveman days, men hunted together in silence so that they wouldn't warn and scare off their prey. Women, however, stayed in the cave watching their children or gathering food and, with absolutely no reason to be quiet, they bonded over conversations about where to pick the best berries and how appalling that new cave girl is with her too-short fur minis. . . .

The result of all that yadda, yadda, yadda?

Women's brains became highly evolved in speech and language functions—as a matter of fact, studies show that women have a verbal output of around 7,000 words a day. Men? A mere 3,000. And you know what that means, right?

When he has become verbally spent (or what I call "vocabu-weary"), you still have at least another 4,000 words to say to meet your verbal quota. With that in mind, is it any wonder he resorts to a caveman's grunt in response to your "How was your day?" queries?

Which leads me to ponder . . . we live in a world where it's primarily *men* leading countries and *men* trying to form relationships with each other through communication . . . in 3,000 words or less. And we wonder why there's such a lack of understanding between nations?

But I digress.

RelationTip: If you want to drive your point home with a man, never take the scenic route.

Back when we were first discussing the two-headed being concept, I told you that, while we couldn't completely change the smaller-head-as-leader syndrome, we *could* find ways to keep Gray Matter Headquarters engaged longer by making our needs known right up front in a direct manner.

That's exactly the mindset you need to keep when it comes to the non-communication situation between the sexes.

Dating Diary

. . . Greg used to call every day during Happy Days and Laverne and Shirley. We'd keep the phones in our ears and watch together in silence. When I tried to talk during the commercials, he told me to hold on so that he could "do something."

. . . Will was willing to call, just unable to figure out what the heck to say. "Hey, what's up?" "Oh, I went to the mall today and found this amazing dress that I didn't think I could actually afford, but then, when I took it to the register, I found out it was like almost half off." Silence. "So, did you do anything today?"

. . . When Joe was around his friends, the fantasy football conversations were fast and furious. Around me? "So, Joe, how was work?" "Okay." "Your secretary said you were out for lunch—where did you go?" "Some Chinese place." "Oh, was it good? Should we go there?" "I guess so."

. . . Nothing irritated Frank more than when I'd spend the whole day shopping with Karen and then come home to about an hour's worth of phone chat. "You spent the whole day with her—what the hell do you still have to talk about?"

The Non-Communication Situation

I always laugh when I hear that a woman is punishing a man by not talking to him.

Are you *kidding* me?

Why don't you just follow that up with, "That's right, mister. I'm just going to let you lay there with one hand on the remote and a cooler full of beer until you see things my way!"

You and I both know that we probably have a good, oh, four hours max before we're suddenly in a cleaning frenzy that takes us into blocking-his-view–knocking-his-stuff-over territory to force him back into some sort of vocal confrontation.

If this sounds familiar . . . know that you've just had a non-communication confrontation!

The reason behind what just happened is precisely because men *are* converse-adverse and we're just the opposite . . . just one of many non-communication situations we will review below.

+ Men speak when they have something to say. Women talk as a way of forming closer, deeper bonds with people they care about.

+ Men like to talk about solutions. Women like to talk about the process without necessarily having to come up with a final answer.

+ Men talk about personal problems in general terms. Women will supply nitty-gritty details.

+ Men try to overcome a stressful situation by concentrating on some other activity. Women vent with focus.

+ Men find it extremely hard to apologize. Women apologize constantly.

+ Men hate being asked questions that put them into agonizing, "damned if I'm truthful, damned if I'm not" situations. Women constantly ask questions with no intention of believing the answer.

And the absolute worst non-communication situation:

✦ Men really don't know what you want until you tell them. Women think that if a man truly cares, he doesn't *have* to ask, he just knows.

Know what's really interesting about the non-communication situations?

During those first few dates in the Best Behavior Zone, it's not an issue because you are *both* trying hard to impress each other, read each other's signals, and work together to get to know more about each other.

Then . . . once you've decided that you are mutually Dateworthy, and you move out of the Zone and into the real world, you both stop trying—and start *expecting*—an automatic understanding about communication needs.

It's no biggie for men who are actually glad to kick back on the communication. But it's a huge problem for women, who wonder what happened to the guy who used to enjoy long, late-night conversations.

So how do we fix this so that we don't end up complaining, "We never talk!" to our men who reply, "That's not true—we're talking now!"

First, we review the non-communication situations.

Second, we use them to put potential Dateworthy men in the right direction. Because, believe it or not, men *do* want direction.

Yes, I know all the jokes about how men absolutely don't want to stop and ask for directions. And that's actually true; they don't want to *stop* and ask for directions once they've plotted their course.

Over the years, however, I've gotten hundreds of letters from men—asking for direction. And I had a light-bulb RelationTip moment: Men *will* ask for direction *before* they start on their course of action. Once they've plotted how they are going to get from point A to point B, then . . . well, asking *then* is pretty much like asking them to admit they are *wrong*.

That's right. And being *wrong* is right up there with having to apologize on their top ten hate-to-do list.

Men are sponges right at the beginning of dating, trying to figure out what it is they can do to impress you. And yes, there's the two-headed being agenda in that. However, if you tailor what you ask for with respect to your communication needs around his communication abilities, you'll get him into good communication habits that will be automatic—even beyond the Best Behavior Zone.

Chatter Matters

Now for a little warning: While you're fine-tuning his communication abilities, you're also going to have to temper your own evolutionary-inspired talking tactics. The following is not just about getting him to be more communication-compatible; it's also about getting you to rethink your communication expectations.

> RelationTip: There's nothing that stops a conversation with a man from going anywhere more quickly than the question, "Where is this conversation going?"

Because men are "solution oriented," we're going to solve the diatribe dilemma by mapping out his non-communication situation and following it with a Dateworthy chatter solution.

The Situation: Men speak when they have something to say.

Dating Diary

Rick was very Bruce Willis—a little short on the hairline, but long on per-sonality and a smile that I loved to be the constant recipient of. After a date, we'd call each other and spend at least an hour on the phone, re-capping the evening and how much fun we had. I encouraged him to tell me stories about places he'd been and what he hoped to accomplish in life, and the more he talked, the more I listened . . . and the more I felt that we should just date each other exclusively.

And then, once we started seeing each other on an almost daily basis, we didn't talk. Except, of course, if I asked him about him. He never, ever asked me anything. Well, of course not—he never had to before. Why should he start now? When I tried, he ended up breaking up with me be-cause now my wanting to talk wasn't fun—it was nagging.

The Solution: While men don't just talk for talking's sake, they will feel the need to speak if they are asked a question. Because we talk to form close bonds and to get a deeper understanding of others, we need to ask questions about the things we really want to know. Encouraging men to talk about issues they don't normally bring up makes for men who will feel more comfortable opening up down the road.

The Situation: Men like to talk about solutions.

The Solution: Never start any story about a concern or issue you have by opening with, "I've got this problem . . ." or you may find yourself being interrupted by *his* solution before you ever get to *your* point of view. Guys don't get that you're sharing the emotional twists and turns just for the effect of the story. The way they see it, you are lost and looking for an answer. If he does end up cutting you off and providing his take on a situation, don't think he's being a know-it-all. Remember, it's his nature to be task-accomplished–oriented. Instead, say, "You know, that's a great point. Now let me tell you the rest to see if you change it!" Just watch: a few of those, and next time he'll ask if you're finished before offering up his wisdom.

The Situation: Men talk about personal problems only in general terms.

The Solution: Ever notice that it's never the situation, but rather a small detail—the way someone looked at you, or the one word that cut you to the bone—that really can take you from a rational to an emotional storyteller? It's hard enough for men to open up and admit they have a problem that they haven't yet solved—even worse if it brings out overwhelming emotions that will make them feel like they look weak in their woman's eyes. Let go of the idea that you two will talk a situation inside out, backward and forward to really examine and exhaust every nuance about a personal problem. Do try to help him talk things out and ask questions, but if he's not forthcoming, just let it go and say, "That's okay. Although I like to have someone ask me questions, I totally understand if that's not what you want." By saying that, you've catered to the male non-communication situation *and* have been extremely blunt about what you need when you're upset.

The Situation: Men try to overcome a stressful situation by concentrating on some other activity.

The Solution: Do you know why women, on average, live longer than men? When something bugs us, we hit the speed dial faster than Jennifer Lopez gets another rock and get those ugly, stressful feelings off our chests. Men? They just want to forget it. Move it aside and concentrate on something else until they're ready to look at it again and find a solution to the problem. Talk about an ulcer waiting to happen.

Here's a little secret that one of my past interview subjects, the communication queen Deborah Tannen, told me: While men don't share problems in a sitting-down-let's-talk kind of way, they *do* have a tendency to muse aloud if the talking is not the central activity. In other words, if you see he's upset, get him to help you wash the car or change your blinds or some other project . . . and then casually bring up, "I noticed you seemed like you had a bad day." And say nothing further. He'll talk in bits and pieces—no, no details, but he'll start opening up enough for him to relieve a little of that internal stress. Don't ask questions here—or offer up solutions; otherwise, he'll clam up. Just respond in buddy mode with "Really?", "Oh wow," or "That sucks." The guy who realizes he can say something without being prodded for details opens up more and more on his own. You just have to be patient on this one.

The Situation: Men find it extremely hard to apologize.

The Solution: For whatever reason, saying "I'm sorry" takes a guy back to that one day when someone was being a real bully and forced him into saying "Uncle!" or "I give up!" if he wanted the pain of his arm being twisted to stop. Tough, because for many women, "All I really wanted was an apology," is an ingrained thing. Have you ever noticed that as women, we open lots of sentences with, "I'm sorry, but . . ." ready to apologize whether the person we speak to will actually need it? Right off the bat, on a first date, ask the guy, "Got any pet peeves?" and follow with, "Really? Let me tell you mine," placing "a man who can't apologize" at the top of your list. Just be sure to follow that up with an observation that will help him understand that you view saying sorry as one of the *sexiest* things a man can do. (That's right—you are going to relate *sexy* to being able to say sorry, and Reaction Central is going to make him think twice about that.) Try, "There's nothing that turns me on more than a man who understands that an apology is the key to sexy make-up make-outs." Talk about giving good direction!

The Situation: Men hate being asked questions that put them into agonizing situations.

The Solution: You know what I mean . . . You knew damn well that the girl he glanced at was a *stunner*, but you still had to ask, "Do you think she's prettier than me?" You can tell that the outfit you have on accentuates your extra-ten-pound-carrying behind, but you still inquire, "Does this make me look fat?" This is a totally unacceptable, *undateworthy* conversation that has nothing to do with communication and everything to do with ego boosting. Do not ask leading questions that you already know the answers to. If you *need* a shot to your self-worthfullness, just come right out and ask for what you want: "Man, I sure could use a compliment right now." And allow *him* to come up with something you might not have asked for, but which could be surprisingly pleasant just the same.

The Situation: Men really don't know what you want until you tell them.

The Solution: Remember how you had to write a letter to Santa telling him what you wanted for Christmas? And how happy you were to get most—if not all—of everything you wished for?

Santa is a *man*, sweetie. Let this be your open-up direction in the future: If you don't get into the habit of coming right out and talking about what would make *you* happy, the men you date will always come up lacking. I know it's a female thing to believe that

Dating Diary

Once Eric started his night job, it was really hard for us to spend serious, quality time together. As a matter of fact, on the one day he had off—Sunday—we'd end up doing a whole lot of nothing after he'd sleep in late. Oh, sure, we'd plan on doing things, but once I got there, or he got to my place, somehow we'd end up sitting on the couch, holding hands in front of the TV. I wanted to be understanding—there're few things I like more than a man who has a real work ethic—so I didn't say anything about the couch time. One Sunday, he told me his friends were picking him up to go to the football game—would I be okay with that? "Oh . . . that's okay," I said, seething inside.

Two weekends later, another game and a "I work so much I rarely see my friends either!"

I said, "Fine," instead of, "Are you crazy? We barely see each other as it is!"

And when he broke up with me a few weeks later? "I like you but . . . we never did anything but sit on the couch, and things were getting stale."

men can look deep into your eyes and read what your soul is longing for. Snap out of it. Santa is a much more realistic communication situation!

Being—and choosing—Dateworthy truly does start, and continue, with being able to communicate with each other. And here are the keys to dating communication:

+ First, you have to find out if he's got the Non-Negotiable goods.

+ Second, you have to ask questions about things that are important to you.

+ Third, you *have to listen.*

+ Fourth, you have to take time to see if what he claims is truly who he is.

+ Fifth, you have to gender-tailor your communication skills, turning the non-communication situation into a talk headed in the right direction.

And speaking of the right direction—let's move forward and check out yet another checklist!

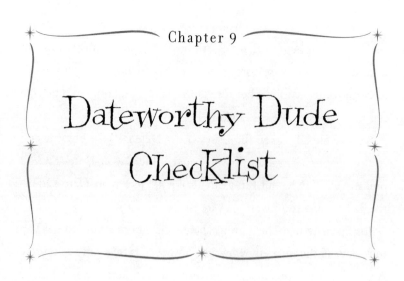

Chapter 9

Dateworthy Dude Checklist

Look at *you*!

You are primed and ready to embark on yet another check-up. But first let's review what you have already aced:

+ You faced the knowledge that you are the common denominator in all your failed relationships.

+ You know that *you* have to be Dateworthy before you can recognize Dateworthy in others.

+ You checked your most-bound-to-be-broken-up-with behaviors at the door and became your Dateworthiest.

+ You learned that just as it was *your* choice to become Dateworthy, it's up to you to *choose* Dateworthy.

Now it's time to see whether you've truly learned how to choose your dates—and better yet, whether you've found the confidence to know that the next time you get the old "It's not you . . . it's *me*!" routine, you'll believe that yes, it's his issues preventing him from fully appreciating your Dateworthiness. You'll have the courage not to compromise yourself because of his hang-ups, and you'll be able send him back to Ye Old Dating Pond.

You've already taken the Dateworthy Defense belt—by the end of this chapter, you'll also have earned a Tae Kwon-Date-Tactical one as well. (Sorry, but I just can't call it a Tae-Kwon-Date-Offensive belt; it just sounds so . . . offensive.)

Just like the first checkup in chapter 5, there's a quiz to get you to review all the new guy why-and-how secrets that you've secured. Acing it doesn't mean that you've learned to actually *think* like a guy . . . just that you have a handle on what he's thinking. (Just as a guy uses our on-our-sleeve romanticism to get what he wants . . . use this information to get what *you* need!) There's also a list that you should consider keeping in your bag to go over in the ladies room at the end of the date to help you decide if you're going to actually exchange more personal contact information.

RelationTip: Always carry a bag big enough for your cell phone, your keys, your lipstick, money, your credit card, and your checklists—you'll be prepared for anything.

And then there's the bonus: The "How to Know He's Just Not Interested" Troubleshooter Guide, *your* definitive list of *dis* (disinterested, disengaged, dismissive . . .), the three little letters that mean never, ever hearing those three little words that make every girl swoon. (No. I don't mean "You look svelte." I mean "I love you.")

Pens up, eyes down. Circle true or false. No fair peeking at the answers!

The Quiz

T F 1. Communication begins at Reaction Central.

T F 2. Gray Matter Headquarters cannot override the small, but powerful, Reaction Central.

T F 3. You can completely change a man from acting as a two-headed being.

T F 4. Men love sex.

T F 5. Men often dispute the answers to relationship quizzes.

T F 6. It's okay to change your dating rules according to the man you're dealing with.

T F 7. Men believe in fairy tales.

T F 8. Trailer Talk is trashy.

T F 9. Men don't want relationships—just sex.

T F 10. Salvageable men are always Dateworthy—you just need to do some more work to get them there.

T F 11. You should date only one guy at a time so that you can focus on his behavior.

T F 12. The only bad guy behavior you are responsible for is the one you nag him into.

T F 13. A good woman is one that helps a man when he's down, out, and addicted.

T F 14. Shopping for a guy is a lot like outlet shopping.

T F 15. If a man is really jealous, it's because he's really into you.

T F 16. A man has less than half the amount of a woman's verbal output ability.

T F 17. If you want to drive home your point with a man, never take the scenic route.

T F 18. Men communicate deeply with other men but not with women.

T F 19. The Best Behavior Zone is the best time to figure out a guy's true feelings.

T F 20. Men don't take direction.

T F 21. Women are the great communicators; it's up to men to completely change the way they talk and listen.

T F 22. Giving a guy the silent treatment is considered cruel and unusual punishment.

T F 23. It's okay to have sex on the first date if he displays all the very important Non-Negotiable behaviors.

T F 24. Dating is a numbers game.

T F 25. All the good ones are taken.

Answers

1. False. Reaction Central is merely the processing area of Gray Matter Headquarters—without the brain, it's really got no game.

2. False. If a guy really likes you—and is given a sense of direction as to where you want this relationship to go—he can override the Reaction Central drive.

3. False. Men are extremely visual—and sexual. While you can keep him from treating you like some kind of sexual object—and take your thoughts and feelings seriously—you can't stop him from imagining you as one (French maid outfit and handcuffs, anyone?).

4. True. I so gave you that one!

5. False. Men don't even *read* relationship quizzes.

6. False. You need to have a set of rules and regulations (remember the Non-Negotiables?) that you consistently live by, not one that changes according to the guy. Change the requirements too often, and soon you'll forget them as well.

7. True. The good ones believe that a woman worth having is a woman they must slay dragons for.

8. False. Trailer Talk is essential in setting up the dating scenario that you want. *You* need to take the trash *out* of it to keep his mind from picturing you in trashy lingerie later.

9. False. Every guy does want a relationship; he just doesn't put it in the priority section of his To Do list.

10. False. Salvageable men are only Dateworthy if *they* are willing to do some work.

11. False. Everyone is on his/her best behavior for the first few months, so you need to date several guys during this period

to avoid wasting valuable time on one that may not even be close to Dateworthy.

12. False. *You* are responsible for the nagging—not for his reaction to it. Any guy who blames *you* for ugly behavior needs to be sent packing. And do be kind enough to warn him not to let the door hit him in the behind on the way out.

13. False. If you are in a long-term, committed marriage, being supportive is expected. When you're dating, however, that's most-bound-to-be-broken-up-with behavior known as the Rescuer. Remember: Dependent does not equal Dateworthy.

14. True. Your shopping list is your man plan. Where you choose to shop is a place you know quality goods can be found. You take your time really checking out sizes and seams to see if you are truly getting a great deal. And, of course, you bring more than one item into the fitting room!

15. False. Jealousy is all about insecurity. If you feel the need to make him jealous in order to feel wanted, that's Drama Queen behavior—and you need some serious Dateworthy self-work. If he's jealous over everything you do, that's a cautionary clue that needs your immediate attention and assessment. Trust your gut. If his jealousy is making you even the slightest bit uncomfortable, and mentioning it makes it worse, get rid of him.

16. True. A paltry 3,000, compared to about 7,000.

17. True. Get right to the point. With him, I mean.

18. False. Men may talk to a buddy about things that bother him, but he doesn't lay it all out there the way women do with each

other. As a matter of fact, he'd be too afraid that doing so would make him look like a wuss in his friends' eyes, and *you'd* have a better shot at getting more details than his buds would.

19. False. He's being the best he can be—and guess what? So are you. Enjoy this gorgeous, flirtatious fun time and then . . . after a few months, see whether, as reality creeps in, he still hasn't turned creepy.

20. False. They love direction—that is, as long as it's given to them at the beginning of the ride. Anytime after that and it becomes orders.

21. False. Yes, we are the great communicators, and any researcher or brain scan you have will prove that we have the superior skills. Because of that, however, we need to adjust our way of connecting when it comes to vocabuweary men so that we can enable them to have spurts of meaningful conversation.

22. True. For *you*, that is.

23. False. And I mean *soooo* very false! It doesn't matter how amazing someone seems on a first date. Being that intimate on a first date—the best behavior pinnacle—is never, *ever* a good (or Dateworthy) idea.

24. True. Men who know their worth know that they have the luxury of taking their time to make the best choice possible— and they date a lot to make sure that they haven't missed out on someone who could end up being their most Dateworthy woman of all.

25. False. It's especially false now that you know your own self-worthfullness!

Check Your Knowledge
Review Checklists

Before you get carried away by that next pretty face (at this point, you and I both know that this will be followed by a Depp reference), I want you to review and renew your determination *not to think that a man thinks like a woman.*

These are bottom-line, Guy'd-lines, my friend. Make them your *man*-tra!

The Whys of Guys

Men are two-headed beings:

+ Gray Matter Headquarters is the larger head where all messages enter.

+ Reaction Central is the smaller, but no less powerful, head where all messages are decoded into sex.

Rewire Gray Matter Guy'd-lines:

+ Men love sex. Make it clear that you do not have sex on the first date.

+ Men are visual. Dress prettily, not provocatively.

+ Men believe in fairy tales.

+ Be a challenge.

+ Men will forego sex for ego attention. Compliment him in the two areas most important to him: let him know you find him attractive and his job interesting.

+ Men do want relationships. It's just not their priority—and on the first two or three dates, that shouldn't be on your mind either.

Recognize Good, Bad, and Salvageable

Good habits:

+ Look for the Non-Negotiables.

+ Take your time. You don't want to rush into deciding if a guy is a good one, especially since he's in his Best Behavior Zone for the first few months.

+ Date more than one guy at a time.

Bad guy signposts:

+ Lies

+ Cheating

+ Neglect

+ Abuse

+ Addiction

Salvageable border issues:

+ Insecurity

+ Sexually charged conversation

+ Ego-overdose

+ Constant comedian

+ Jealousy

Revise Your Communication Consciousness

Men can and do become vocabuweary. Women have a verbal output of 7,000 words a day compared to a man's mere 3,000.

Men have non-communication situations:

+ They speak only when they have something to say.

+ They are solution-answer–oriented.

+ They talk about personal problems in general terms.

+ They equate saying "I'm sorry" to crying "*Uncle!*"

+ They internalize their issues instead of talking them out.

+ They hate those "Does this make me look fat?" and other impossible, no-win question situations women put them into.

+ They aren't mind readers and like to be *told* what it is that you need from them.

Now let's move on to a section that I think is really important.

How to Know He's Just Not Interested (And Other Troubleshooter Tips)

Why are these tips so important?

Because being a "Dateworthy double" does not necessarily mean you two will be a team. It's possible that while he is extremely

Dateworthy and obviously in full recognition of just how Dateworthy *you* are, you just can't get beyond that no-sparks friendship feeling.

Unfortunately, that can also happen the other way around. And when it does . . . very often, as women, we try to read between the lines of what he's saying and what he's doing and what we *want* it all to mean.

So, here's a list of troubleshooter tips. If you notice any of these behaviors or changes in your guy: no making up excuses to make everything okay. Okay? You need to let him go . . . and say *so what?* And remember that no door closes without another one opening up, and most often, it leads to something even better. Like . . . you know . . . a Dateworthy doubles team that wins championships.

1. **He doesn't initiate contact.** There are about a million and seven ways people can connect these days and absolutely zero excuses why he cannot reach out and touch (exception: He has just become a missionary and left for a six-month tour in countries where one must use leaves for toilet paper). If he's not calling—or returning calls—you are *not* on his brain (or anywhere else for that matter).

2. **He doesn't make plans.** If he cannot commit as far down the road as say, this weekend, it's because he's hoping for something better to take up his time.

3. **He talks about his ex all the time.** Constant ex-rated talk means that his heart and interests are still with her—and you are nothing but the temporary rebound chick.

4. **He keeps his cell phone on when he's with you and off when he's not.** Everybody else can get a hold of him when

he's with you, but somehow *you* can never get him to pick up—unless you are on someone else's phone line and then he apologizes, makes small talk, and ooops—he's got another call to take.

5. **He doesn't try to make you happy.** As a matter of fact, he doesn't go the extra mile at all with respect to complimenting your appearance or taking care of his. He's even a little mean, a little sarcastic, a little short on patience. Hate to say it, but he's hoping you break up with him so that he doesn't have to do it.

So, what are you going to do with all that knowledge?

Glad you asked.

You're going to utilize it on your next first date with some help from the next few chapters.

intelligent **Part 3**

open-minded responsible

funny *self-aware*

Dating 101

trusting sexy

magnetic

self-respecting

confident

passionate

Chapter 10

"Meet" Markets

What do you mean, you can't meet anyone?

Unless you're a complete and total homebound hermit with no family and friends and who doesn't have access to a phone, computer, or television, I find that hard to believe.

Venture outside, and you chance bumping into someone who could end up being the love of your life. Friends and family are invaluable for fix-ups. Organized social situations—like church, school, and the gym—abound with singles. Don't feel like leaving your house? Turn on your computer, and check out a dating site or interesting chat. Open a magazine or newspaper and peruse the personals. Tune in to a dating show and call their toll-free number to be fixed up on national television.

With so many options and opportunities available, there's no reason why you can't meet potential love interests. So, what's holding you back?

I know it's *not* because you lack the confidence in your Date-worthiness.

Oh, wait . . . Did you say, "Just *clueless*?" Well, then, pack up that Good Luggage and get ready to explore! Let's take a look at ways to get yourself on the "Meet" Market.

Fate Dates

The fate date occurs merely by your staying open and being friendly every time you leave the house. Fate dates can happen with very little effort: Catch someone's eye at the grocery store and smile. Ask a cutie a question about a bottle of wine or a publication that he's skimming through at the bookstore. Head out to a local street fair, community block party, anything that gets you out of the house and gives you a reason to mingle with others.

RelationTip: If you choose to head to a bar, go at happy hour—the evening bar and club scene is way too competitive, shallow, and noisy for real conversation.

Keep in mind that the best fate dates happen when you're attending something that you have a huge interest in. Meeting someone at a language class, wine tasting, or a music festival gives you an automatic something-in-common to talk about. (And hey, even if you didn't meet the someone to steal your heart, you've enriched your life in other ways!) My favorite: Volunteer! You'll help others and meet people like yourself—with big hearts.

Dating Diary

Fate dates can happen anywhere and everywhere—while doing errands, shopping, working out; attending neighborhood events, church, classes; volunteering, or even keeping a friend company while she's making her daily rounds! Here are a few of mine.

. . . Going on a mid-morning, iced coffee run to a nearby deli, I ran into Matt, who was running late to his job—he bought my coffee in exchange for the digits. . . .

. . . Went shopping with my mom for an outfit for a dance I didn't have a date to. As I passed the shoe store, I noticed the cutest sales guy and detoured in. Bill tried to sell me an evening bag—I said it was too small to fit all my stuff. He made a bet that everything would fit or he'd take me to the dance. It didn't . . . so he did . . .

. . . Walking my basset hound, I bumped into—and then was tangled with—Bob and his golden retriever. . . .

. . . At the dentist's office for my wisdom-tooth surgery follow-up, and looking like hell. Ron was sitting across from me, and when he caught my eye, I convinced myself to talk to him anyway. I said, "You know, I don't always look like I just went ten rounds. . . ." and he laughed.

The Fix-Up

Aaah, the family and friend fix-ups. One might think that this would be a whole lot less scary than flinging yourself into the winds of fate.

Not exactly.

Sure, the fix-up does seem to have a kind of built-in safety feature (the potential date and your friend or family member know each other, thus the odds that he's a serial killer or panty stealer are pretty low). That small measure of comfort, however, comes with some strings attached:

+ If the guy is a major creep, you can't just throw a drink in his face or excuse yourself to the bathroom, intending to make a hasty escape out the window. Well, you could, but then you'll have to answer to the friend or family member who fixed you up.

+ If you don't click with at least three family fix-ups, the gossip grapevines will have you pegged as a "difficult, picky, doomed old maid." That's right—their bad choices will be *your* fault.

+ If the fix-up is absolutely crushed by your disinterest, you could end up having to deal with your friend's wrath—or renewed determination to get you both together (aka: every time you socialize, he'll just happen to show up).

I'm not saying that the fix-up is not a viable option. The fix-up can actually lead to some pretty amazing dates and even long-term romance with the Dateworthy dude of your dreams. The reason why so many people run into snags with the fix-up is that they mistakenly give full control of the situation over to the well-meaning matchmakers.

If you want the fix-up to be added to your dating arsenal, keep the following in mind:

+ Narrow your field of aspiring Cupids. A little trial and error will tell you who truly knows you, and who is just fixing you

Dating Diary

My friend Amy was always talking about setting up her very best friend, James, with me. She showed me a few pictures and, yes, he was pretty cute, so I agreed to go out with him.

The only thing we had in common: We both thought he was pretty hot. James spent the evening talking about himself in the third person. Catching his reflection in store mirrors as we walked down the street. Letting me know just how nice it was to find a woman who didn't talk about herself all night. Heck, I couldn't get a word in edgewise if I tried and gave silent kudos to the woman who actually did.

At the end of the night, I gave him a hug, said good night, and deleted his digits.

Amy called the next day, raving about how much James loved me. "You have no idea—he is just soooo picky, and I've never seen him so into someone!"

Yikes! I lied and told her that I had a great time, but that I really didn't want to date anyone exclusively right now.

She begged me to change my mind. Pleaded her case, letting me know that she was on her knees on the uneven cement floor area by her phone table, bleeding for the cause.

I said maybe.

I avoided his calls and then realized I had to screen and avoid hers as well—sometimes she'd call and have him on the other line. Every time we planned to go out, he'd show up. I rewarded his persistence with one more date. I had such a lousy time, I told him not to call me anymore.

He didn't, and neither did Amy.

up without any thought process except, "Gee, he's single, and she's single . . . they're *perfect* for each other!"

+ Don't enter the date blindly. It's the computer age, baby. Insist that the fix-up needs to do a little pre-date corresponding via e-mail, picture exchange included.

+ If you didn't have a good time, admit it to the friend who fixed you up, but do so with a compliment: "Yes, he's really cute, and I'm so flattered you thought of me for him, but he and I just don't have anything in common." Period. And never say *maybe* if it's really *hell, no!*

+ Strike a no-pressure deal with your fixer-upper. If things don't work, they won't hold it against you. If things *do* work, they'll stay out of it.

Every once in a while, it's okay to live a little dangerously and go out on a traditional, sight-unseen fix-up (that is, if the source is someone you respect). Giving up control every once in a while is healthy, and even if it's not a love match, it just may be a great new friendship or business contact.

Personal Proactivity

You're getting out more, seeing and being seen. You're letting friends and family know that you are willing to explore fix-ups. That is a huge step in a Dateworthy direction!

But if you really, truly want to take charge of your dating life—and move beyond the regular faces, places, and social circles—it's time to get proactive and investigate some of the more modern meeting methods.

RelationTip: Skip professional matchmakers unless you've got megabucks to drop—huge fees with no real guarantees.

Singles-Specific Soirees

The dance, the sporting event, the cruise, the cocktail parties. There are lots of affordable or free organized events for the single set, easily located via your local paper and online. Some are gimmicky (superdark restaurants where you are forced to chat with singles you can't see, thus giving the not-so-hot a shot); other are more straightforward fun. Mingle with random singles, or look for get-togethers that cater to certain characteristics (like Jewish singles and single parent events).

RelationTip: Attend events sponsored by several different organizations. If you end up breaking up with someone from one particular group, you'll avoid running into that new ex.

Speed-Dating

Whether it's called eight-minute dating or the three-minute mingle, the premise is the same: A restaurant, club, or café will host a speed-dating event where a small group of singles—evenly divided between men and women—are given "score" cards, conversations are timed, the buzzer rings, and you move on to the next table. Lather, rinse, repeat. At the end of the night, you turn in your cards. If the people you chose have also chosen *you* as someone they'd like to see again, the speed-dating coordinator facilitates the exchange of contact info. Depending on the timing, length of the event, and amount of people, you could possibly have a sit-down with a good twelve to fifteen people in one night!

Speed-dating is fun, especially if you go with a friend and compare conversations (the guy who told you he was an airline pilot told your friend that he was a fashion photographer, or you realize the guy you both liked told the same story and joke, word for word). You should also go in with the realization that the shorter the timing, the less you'll be able to share what's meaningful, and the more choices will be made on physical attraction.

Speed-dating can be tough on people who can't think that fast under pressure. Coming prepared with your top three most important Non-Negotiables (Some good ones: Are you a smoker? Have you ever been arrested? Do you have a job? Do you live with your mother?) and a funny one-liner that sums you up pretty well (something a little deeper than "Never eats carbs and hates when the toilet seat is left up.") will up your partner potential.

RelationTip: Don't write someone off just because they aren't as quick-witted or slick as some of the other participants—the guy who is fumbling may be more sincere.

Personals Ads

Whether it's via your local paper, a magazine, or an online dating site, writing—and responding to—personals ads is the ultimate proactive, take-charge-of-your-dating-destiny option. To sell yourself, you really do have to dig up the good stuff—the things that truly make you more than just the size of your thighs. Know that old saying, "You can't really love someone else until you can love yourself"? Personals ads help you connect to you, and hopefully, that enthusiasm and confidence will attract a like-minded someone!

There're two ways to do the personals. Write your own ad, and wait for others to respond to you, or, the better, proactive approach: Place your profile, and respond to others' as well. Now let's take a look at how to put together an effective ad.

> RelationTip: Invite several friends over for an ad-writing party—you supply the wine and fun food, they come with their own ideas of what you should include in your ad.

+ Be clear about your Non-Negotiables. If you absolutely hate smokers or guys who live for monster truck races, say so. The clearer you are about what you don't want, the more tailored-to-you your responses will be.

+ Get to the point. The last thing a man wants to do is wade through a long-winded giant dissertation that reads like a psychiatric evaluation. ("I am a woman who knows what she wants and while some men may find that intimidating, I would imagine that having a can-do attitude would be refreshing. . . ." Snooze. Next.) When I write a RelationTips column, my goal is to get in and out with as much important information in limited space as possible. In that spirit, aim for around 135 words in print (that's about the length of this tip), and structure it so that 75 percent is about you, 25 percent about what you want in a man.

+ Make it fun! Don't just name your qualifications in a laundry list that reads, "I am smart and have an interest in martial arts." Instead, say, "I am more Buffy than Jessica Simpson!"

+ Watch what you call yourself. Giving yourself a name like "2Hot2Handle," "Stuftanimalgrl," or "Nutcracker" can and will make a first impression that you may not intend and stop a guy from reading any farther. Keep it simple—just your name and a few numbers (date of birth, the number of your gym locker, whatever).

+ Spell-check! Typos are a turnoff. Use your computer's spell-check function, and then have a friend go over it once more to catch any missed words (you typed "an" when you meant "and").

+ Post a photo. Hands down, the ads with photos get the hugest response. And make sure it's a smile shot: Studies show that photos of people who look like they're relaxed and having fun get more positive attention. Be sure to use a *recent* photo and to have a trusted friend or two let you know if it's flattering but looks like you. Consider paying a friend who's good with a camera to shoot two or three rolls of you—the more shots you have to choose from, the better your odds will be of finding the best representation of you.

And now that your ad is up and running, don't waste that waiting time—start responding!

I know that when I used to respond to the personals, I preferred to answer ads in *New York Magazine*, where people who placed ads were paying around $35 a line—I figured, if they were shelling out *that* kind of dough, they were serious about a relationship. (I also figured they'd be able to afford to take me to fabulous places. . . .) Beyond *New York*, I tried out the music magazine personals—after going out with a *NYM* millionaire, I didn't mind doing the occasional struggling musician thing.

The worst experiences? Daily newspaper personals. Somehow, newspaper personals people always seemed sloppy, weird, and really pushy about having sex. Avoid 'em. (Unless of course, I've just described *your* ultimate type. . . .)

The downside of print personals: For the most part, they do not include a picture. So, read the ads with a healthy bit of skepticism with respect to how a guy describes his physical being. I cannot tell you how many times a "Tom Cruise type" showed up, and the only thing he and Tom shared in the looks department were a lack of height and a big nose.

What's more important is to pay attention to what he likes to do, and what he's looking for in a woman, and be as honest as you can about fitting that description. (If you are short and allergic to cats, don't answer an ad looking for a willowy feline lover, no matter how amazing this guy sounds.) I know, I know, you think, "If he just got the opportunity to *know* me, he'd throw that old criteria right out the window." I say, how would *you* like it if the tables were turned and some guy you didn't describe wasted *your* time?

Now let's talk about online ads. Although it's possible to connect in a "chat room" (translation: You enter a chat, find that you are connecting with one person more than the other chat respondents, and you two agree to go to another chat area to get to know each other without distractions), I'm not a huge fan of the method. While meeting in, let's say, a Yanni chat room means you both already share something in common, it's not as secure as meeting on a dating site. Also, your odds of meeting a married, lying somebody are considerably higher.

My advice? Choose an official online dating site over a chat room, particularly one which has a huge, varied membership and is extremely secure—meaning, your personal information remains *private* until you choose to share it. Try several different sites to up your chances of connecting.

Most online ads have one or more pictures, but again, you should remain Ms. Skeptic—those pics may be old or ultra-flattering. (Can you imagine someone doing that?) So, just as with print ads, spend more time on his personality and preferences, and be honest about whether you are truly the dream girl he's describing (if your friends tend to describe you as "unrealistic," you may want to run the ad past one or two of 'em just to be sure).

Once you've chosen your future husband (kidding!) and are ready to reply either in print or online, keep these things in mind:

+ Make your reply stand out. Does his print personal mention that he loves walks on the beach? Enclose a little plastic bag of beach sand with a drink umbrella. Does his online ad say he has a thing for travel? Include some links to exotic locales. Taking the time to be a little creative in response to his "like list" will make him respond to *your* letter first.

+ When responding to a print ad, use nice paper. You don't have to use fancy, personalized stationery or hire a calligrapher; printer compatible paper in a good stock and color that says *you* shows respect for the process.

+ If responding online, use an interesting font. I'm a Comic Sans person—it's easy to read, and the softer, more rounded lettering feels like me! Skip colors that are too bright or light, as well as colored backgrounds—you'll look like you're trying too hard.

Dating Diary

His name was Jay, and his ad said that he was a tall, good-looking private investigator. We met at a downtown restaurant, where there was a tall guy at the bar, but . . . good-looking? Well . . . perhaps if he was in an aquarium. My God, he looked just like a flounder! No chin, waddle down to his collar. . . . and obnoxious as anything. I spent what seemed like an eternity in hell listening to his "I'm the world's best investigator" stories and then opted to get out.

"Jay," I said, "I'm not feeling well. Would you mind giving me cab fare to go home?"

"No," he said. "I'll drive you."

"No," I insisted. "I don't feel comfortable having someone I just met drop me home."

"Don't be ridiculous," he said. "I'm a private investigator—if I wanted to find you, I could. Let's go."

We went to the coatroom and he couldn't find his car keys in his pocket. I waited about five minutes while he verbally abused the coat check girl and then said, "Listen, Magnum P.I., if you can't afford cab fare, I'll just take the bus." He angrily pulled out a twenty. I took the bus anyway and pocketed the change.

Safety First

Now that you know what the Meet Markets are, it's time to go over something really important: staying safe.

While being friendly and approachable is a great way to meet guys on fate dates and reaching out to strangers at singles events or via personals can be fun and lead to romance, they also leave you open to meeting some not-so-savory characters.

What amazes me? The very women who say they don't do on-line dating because they are afraid there's a creep at the other end of the computer correspondence will throw caution to the wind when the great-looking guy they've known only a few hours offers them a ride home; women who won't hesitate to tell an employee their work stinks, but squash the instinct to say "I'm outta here" with a guy who makes their skin crawl in an effort not to look like a bitch; women who don't trust their gut, and who take more time shopping for shoes than jumping into something with men. I'm the first to admit I have, in the past, made some really dumb moves . . . but I was lucky enough to get out of and learn from those situations—and share them with you.

Here's my personal safety checklist:

+ Give out personal contact information sparingly. I used to pay a phone service around ten bucks a month for a number that I could give out that could not be traced back to my home. Having a "throwaway" free e-mail address (Hotmail, Yahoo, etc.) allows you to be contacted without having to worry about someone having access to your main account.

+ Never have someone new pick you up at your home or work. If this guy ends up being someone you want nothing to do with after your first date, you don't want him knowing where he can find you. Have at least three dates before home/work pickups and drop-offs.

+ Always let others know about your date. Tell a friend where you're going, whom you're going with, and what time you expect

Dating Diary

. . . I met P.J. on campus, and after being challenged by his teasing ("What, are you afraid that I'm an axe murderer?"), I went up to his apartment with him just to "hang out a bit and talk" before going home. My gut was saying no, but I went anyway. When we got in, he excused himself and came back a few minutes later with a leather-and-zipper mask, a whip, and ropes. He told me to get down on my knees, and I told him that while I was truly turned on, I had to take a rain check because I had a really bad yeast infection. Heart hammering, I smiled and left calmly . . . and then ran like a crazy person out of the building.

. . . I talked to Josh a few times on the phone after answering his ad and agreed to have him meet me at my job. He was very cute, but after a few dates, I realized that he was extremely needy and found his "I love you so much" confessions too much, too soon, too scary. I told him I had met someone else, and he was, at first, very persistent (calling and sending flowers to the job every day, coming by to talk to me at the end of the work day, etc.). When I finally told him to leave me alone, he threatened to kill himself and then started threatening me. I filed a report with the police and quit my job. The messages on my service number (the first number I gave him) finally stopped.

to be back home. Make a pact with friends: After a first date, you will call and leave a message on a machine, confirming that all is well.

+ Never leave your beverage unattended. If you don't want to bring your drink with you into the bathroom, order a fresh one when you get back. The last thing you need is for someone to slip you a date rape drug.

+ Don't answer questions that make you uncomfortable. If he asks you how much money you make, brings up sexually charged topics, or invades your personal space in a way that bothers you, tell him. The second time he does it, leave, and lose his number.

+ Always check behind you. Whether walking or driving, be sure you're not being followed, *especially* if you've already decided this guy isn't for you.

+ Bring a cell phone.

+ Avoid recreational drugs or any alcohol.

+ Trust your gut feelings.

Feeling scared?

Don't be. Feel smart. Savvy. But definitely don't feel scared. You are now aware, armed with knowledge and able to avoid starring in your own Dating Disaster epic!

Now . . . from being proactive . . . to taking precautions . . . we head to some pre-date prepping!

Chapter 11

Pre-Date Prep

It's the Dennie Theory of Relation-tivity: *Becoming* Dateworthy plus the ability to *choose* Dateworthy multiplied by Meet Marketability equals . . . a date. Several, actually, if you remember to factor in the "it's a numbers game" rule.

Go ahead. Gloat. Pose in the mirror in your underwear and shake it like Cameron Diaz. I'll even join you in a little singsong moment: "I've got a *daa*-aate, I've got a *daa*-aate!"

Now breathe. Settle down, but keep that happy energy up enough to put yourself into pre-date prep mode.

Oh, come on. You didn't expect to just . . . just *go* on a date without any kind of preparation, did you?

Be serious, *woman!*

There's a reason why so many Dateworthy women you know end up all alone doing that cable rerun marathon of *Sex and the City*. It's because they do all the self-work, but then forget to men-

Dating Diary

He played guitar for one of the hottest artists at the time—a real sex idol, if you will. We met at a café on Eighth Street—he caught my eye, and I made my puckering-up-my-lips move at him. He asked me to come to his table, and I ran over, leaving two of my girlfriends in the dust.

The drinks were flowing—and some other not-so-legal stuff as well—so in order to look cool for this guy and not compromise my no-drugs policy, I kept drinking. And drinking. To the point where I totally knew I was drunk . . . but the drinking and the attention and the knowledge that I had on some serious sexy underwear was such a darn turn-on. We walked back to his place and we proceeded to make out in a frenzy that got even more intense when he saw the black lace bra.

Suddenly feeling the cold air on my now shirtless skin—and still keeping my "no sex on a first date" policy firmly in mind (actually, I fuzzily realized that this didn't even qualify as a first date, just a pick-up)—I got sober and tried to slow things down. "Wait," I said and tried to push the red lipstick–smeared face from mine.

"Just relax," he said, pulling me back in with one arm, the other hand practicing some serious guitar techniques all over.

tally and physically prepare for the actual big game . . . and they *choke.* I'm talking, major-league mess-up.

You've come a long way—too far just to throw all caution to the wind and wear those ultrahigh heels that look great but have a no-pain limit of about twenty minutes, to then drink way too many Cosmos and ultimately find yourself doing that walk of shame home

"Wait . . . how about we talk for a while and get to know each other?" He pulled away and looked at me with disgust.

"What the f*ck are you talking about?"

"Um . . . let's talk. How about I make some breakfast?" (I couldn't believe that came out of my mouth. An offer to cook for him? What a loser!)

He sat still and stared at me for the longest moment, then pulled up his leather pants and said, "I'm going back to the bar. But first I'm going to jerk off and you can either watch or get the f*ck out now." I walked out and realized that somehow my money and keys had fallen out of my purse. So I rang the bell and he didn't answer. I waited and twenty minutes later, he walked out and looked at me and said, "Change your mind?" I told him I didn't have any money. He said, "So that's what this was all about? F*ck off."

I ended up walking home, ringing my bell, and waking my roommates at around 4:00 A.M. . . . and when I went to the bathroom, I caught sight of a face smeared with red lipstick and mascara shadows under the eyes. Yuck.

---

at 3:00 A.M., shoes in hand and looking about as used as you feel.

Okay. That's the worst-case scenario.

But we've all had a variation on that theme, haven't we? I say, it's time to put a stop to those scary scenarios. And I'm just the kind of girl who will show you how to do it . . . with some pre-date prep points.

But first, you've got some reviewing to do.

+ Revisit your Check Yourself Checkup to remind yourself what it takes to be your most ultimate Dateworthy self.

+ Refresh your very important Enlist to Resist team and man plan.

+ Reassess your Dateworthy Dude Checklist to brush up on the concept of the two-headed being. (All together now: "Even during the Best Behavior Zone, he's thinking less about relating and more about copulating.")

+ Re-instill the Non-Negotiables.

+ Re-sink those scary signposts into your brain.

And finally . . . incorporate a few more stages, or pre-date prep categories. Let's add to your Dateworthy arsenal!

Clothes Calls

You already know that dressing for the two-headed being should be more pretty than provocative, right?

Now I'm going to give you a cold, hard truth about the call you make on the clothes for that first date: One man's "How lovely!" is often another man's "I'm getting *lucky!*"

Just because you cannot fully control what turns him on doesn't mean you cannot control where this situation goes and take responsibility for how much sex appeal you add to the mix.

1. Be prepared with your Trailer Talk ("This movie is strictly G-rated, buddy") to keep Gray Matter Headquarters from sending too many stimulating visuals to Reaction Central.

Dating Diary

Jake was a personal trainer at my gym whom I finally asked out ("for a coffee or smoothie or whatever?") after a month of barely-there working out on the cardio machines (to avoid that red-faced, sweating look that most guys don't find attractive). We did the juice bar thing a few times, and he finally asked me if I'd like to go dancing at a favorite Spanish-salsa place, and I couldn't wait. I wore a pretty dress—not too low cut, sleeveless to show off my toned shoulders, not too short but swingy and colorful—and a pair of really pretty strappy sandals.

When he picked me up and looked me up and down, he seemed extremely . . . excited. When we got in the cab, he asked me to cross my foot so that he could check out my shoes. I got nervous as I noticed . . . his pants stretching a bit in the front. As the night wore on, he kept reaching for my feet, rubbing them because he said they must hurt from all the dancing, and it was obvious he was getting more excited.

At the end of the night, he walked me to my apartment and begged, "Please . . . can I just come in for a while?" with a full-frontal flag salute.

I said no—firmly—and then I said, "Jake, did I give you the wrong impression tonight that I was . . . I don't know . . . leading you on?"

He sighed and said, "It was the shoes. When I saw them, I just thought that you wore them, you know, because you heard that I have a thing for feet. . . ."

2. Avoid the Carnal Clothing Choices:

  ✦ Too tight

  ✦ Too short

  ✦ Too low-cut

  ✦ Too see-through

  ✦ Too revealing in any way

3. Always wear your most comfortable, ugliest support underwear on those first few "down boy!" dates.

Trust me here. There's nothing that feels sexier than a) the confidence of self-worthfullness, and b) the secret knowledge that you're
wearing Victoria's Secret. Combine both with a first date who is an
unbelievable turn-on . . . add a few drinks . . . and voilà! You just
may send signals that you didn't intend . . . or worse, that you fully
intended he tend to!

✦ RelationTip: You're less likely to lose control if you're sporting control tops.

Listen: I'm not saying that having sex means that you are a horrible person. If that's what you truly want to do, go ahead, fog up
those windows, have a ball (no pun intended).

But . . . may I be blunt here? If all you wanted was to get laid—
not to be appreciated, adored, or courted—why did you work so
hard on becoming a person who deserves to be appreciated, adored,
courted . . . in other words, to be Dateworthy?

Bottom line: As a woman, the moment you have sex—and particularly, great sex—you become way more invested in this guy than you should be this early on.

RelationTip: Getting attached too early can make you try to make something work, as opposed to sensibly evaluating if it really is working.

I think that to retain the power of being Choosy—and to keep your self-worthfullness intact—it's important to keep sex as something that's ahead of you . . . something to share when you've given yourself more time to really see if this guy is worth that kind of investment.

That said—keep those support garments on so that you look *better* with clothes on than clothes off!

So . . . what are some good Clothes Call Considerations?

Comfort is key. If it hurts, pinches, rides up, or just makes you feel uncomfortable, you're not going to feel or act your best.

Never-worn is a no-no. If you've never walked in heels, don't try them out now just because he's the first taller-than-you guy you ever dated. I guarantee falling for him will not be the only fall you make. Don't buy something new. Instead, go for an outfit you've been given compliments on and *know* will not wrinkle, run, or show sweat stains.

Look in the mirror. Sounds like such a no-brainer, right? Believe it or not, when a woman is excited and/or pressed for time, she often forgets to take a good look at her look . . . which can lead to leaving the house with an ugly stain or worse—her / her pantyhose. Check yourself from every angle, a

Assess the activity. Be casual for coffee, a dinner. I find that solid colors, well-fitting par simple lines as a base, touched with a little deta fun bag or favorite jewelry) can strike a balance between trying too hard and looking like you just don't care.

One more thing before we move forward: Along with the Clothes Call, there's a Nose Call. That is, *please*—easy on the fragrance! Guys hate being overpowered by scent. The best way to apply is a spritz on the back of the neck (it'll waft forward as your body warms up) or the spritz walk-through (spray a cloud and walk through it).

Can You Hear Me Now?

Just because men don't see ear-to-ear when it comes to communication doesn't mean you shouldn't do a little pre-date conversation deliberation! Your goals here:

+ To ask the kind of questions that can give you a little insight into who he is.

+ To be prepared with your own answers to those questions for the inevitable, "What about you?"

+ To come off as interested—*and* interesting.

RelationTip: If you've got a date that evening, pick up USA Today or other major newspaper that morning. It's a great source for timely topics that aren't just political- or economy-crisis oriented.

Conversation pre-date prep can make the difference between awkward silences and those natural ones that happen because there's food in your mouth. (Well, one *hopes* that there's no chatting during ing. . . .)

Dating Diary

When I went to audition to be a singer for a band, I couldn't help but fall madly for Steve, the lead guitarist. I got the gig and—despite his protests that dating within a band breaks up a band—got asked out. I couldn't wait to see him—and for him to see me—as a civilian! I decided on my cream-colored jeans tucked into cream-colored, baby-suede boots, a gorgeously soft lavender angora sweater . . . and I spent forever and a can of AquaNet getting the hair just right.

He came to pick me up . . . and he was wearing jeans. And boots. I was disappointed but got in the car. And it wasn't until we were deep into some wooded area when I turned to him and said, "Where are we going?" And he said, "Bow shooting." He looked me up and down and said, "Are you okay with that?"

I lasted about twenty minutes—that's how long it took for me to muddy up my boots and provide hair-housing to several bugs and leaves. I got pissed, pissed him off . . . and I ended up a solo act—no Steve, no band.

Let's break down the dos and don'ts of effective date dialogue: the conversation basics, thrillers . . . and killers.

Conversation Basics

Know what you want to know. You're looking for his Non-Negotiability, cautionary clues, and scary signposts.

Listen to—and *look at*—his responses. More than 80 percent of conversation is physical! When you ask a question, look right at him in a friendly manner. You'll not only catch if there's any agitated or nervous mannerisms (eyes or mouth turn downward), but looking directly at a guy makes him feel like the center of attention and encourages him to divulge more than he normally would. Oh, yeah, and you'll also notice if he's starting to fidget, which leads me to . . .

Brief briefly. Tell him a quick, humorous story. Answer a question without a lengthy "this is my life," too-technical explanation. If you want to go out again, don't go on and on and on. . . . Remember: guys glaze faster than you can say "Krispy Kreme."

Conversation Thrillers

Speak softly . . . and clearly. If he's really paying attention, you'll see him leaning in to hear you. Just make sure that when he gets close enough to listen, he can understand what you're saying. Guys love it when you don't sound like one of the guys . . . yet.

Be complimentary. If he's got a great laugh, tell him. Let him know how much you enjoyed his date idea. Remember: If you're not going to sleep with him (you're *not*, *RIGHT*???) you need another way to let him know that there's interest—and the shortest way to a man's heart is through his ego.

Accept compliments. What is it about women that when someone compliments us, we *downplay* it? Guys find the inability to accept—or the negating of—a compliment an extreme turn-off. Trust me on this: If he tells you, "You're pretty," and you say, "No, I'm not," you're essentially a) questioning his judgment, and b) planting the idea that perhaps you're *not* so fabulous. If he says something nice, make like a man and say, "Thank you!"

Be positive about your life. You want this person to be interested in being a part of your life—and to see just how gorgeous you are when you're animated, laughing, and smiling.

✦ RelationTip: If he keeps avoiding a topic that's important to you, ask the question again in a different way: "When was your last relationship?" becomes "How long have you been single?"

Conversation Killers

Interrogation tactics. Question after question after question . . . good *lord*, woman! It's a date, not a criminal investigation! Rapid-fire questions make a guy feel like you're trying to trip him up, and/or you're just running down an internal checklist of general qualifications—not personal qualities. Ask the questions you want to know (family? friends? living situation? job? interests?), wait for an answer, lob a personal observation or question back . . . now *that's* a conversation.

TMI. There *is* such a thing as Too Much Information. He doesn't need to know that your dad is a drunk, you shave your big toes, or that you were called Pumpkin Head in the fourth grade. Edit down your life's reality show to flattering, funny moments if you want a second date.

Hot-button topics. Do you really need to know his views—or passionately express yours—on the president, abortion, or gay rights? That's the stuff you can agree to disagree on later, when you've both established a bond over the important things, like . . . how you will treat each other.

Ex-bingeing and bashing. Blaming your entire breakup on your ex—and then analyzing every detail of it—tells a guy one thing: You are so not over it and are in rebound mode.

Bound-to-be-broken-up-with babble. Biological clocks, wedding fantasies, and "I'm so tired of being single" topics are *soooo* supposed to be an undateworthy thing of the past!

Now that we've dealt with clothes and conversation—the biggest pre-date stress points—we'll run through a virtual potpourri (prep-pourri, if you will) of other pre-date prep processes you'll need to be date-ready.

Pre-Date Prep Countdown

I'm just *giddy* thinking about you getting all primped and prepared to make an impression on your first "If this doesn't work, it's *you* . . . and absolutely *not me*" date!

We both know you're going to look and sound great. Now let's make sure you are also otherwise prepped with my Pre-Date Prep Countdown!

The Night Before

1. Check out tomorrow's weather forecast so that you can adjust your Clothes Call.

2. Try on the outfit you think you'll be wearing and make sure that it looks great.

3. Hands are key, so make sure your nails look good—short with clear polish is the best way to go.

4. Charge that phone!

5. Get good sleep.

That Day

1. I do this *every* morning to relax and unwind: Sit down, close your eyes, focus on your breathing, and don't think of a *darn*

thing . . . just connect with your breathing for about five or six minutes and let go of any day-ahead stress.

2. If you have time, get in a short workout. It'll energize you and offer stress relief.

3. Skip eating or drinking anything that will end up giving you heartburn, gas, bad breath (*no garlic!*), or cause you to crash and burn early in the evening.

4. Hit the cash machine for your two "emergency" twenties.

That Evening

1. Review your Dateworthy and pre-prep lists while your brain is open and fresh.

2. Shower. Get pretty and don't go overboard on makeup, fragrance, or hardening hair products.

3. Pack your date handbag! No, I didn't say "clutch" or "wristlet" or any other teeny-tiny, "I'm going to the Oscars" thing that only holds a lipstick and a breath mint. (Here's a secret for you: Stars have those on the red carpet because they have publicists who lug all the other vitally important star needs in their own larger bags.)

   I'm talking about a *handbag* that goes with any of your possible date outfits and can fit the following: basic makeup (small, mirrored powder compact and small moisturizing lip color); tissues; if you wear contacts, a teeny bottle of drops; a small ID holder that can also handle one credit card and two "emergency" twenties; breath strips (more compact and faster dissolving than mints or gum); a folded-up copy of your Dateworthy Dude Checklist; keys; cell phone.

4. Call your Date Patrol friend of the evening.

Got a lunch or immediately-after-work date?

+ Pack the bulk of your date handbag the night before.

+ Bring—don't wear—your outfit to work to avoid getting stuck
  with pen ink explosions or coffee drip stains.

+ Don't forget to shower after the gym.

+ Go way minimal on makeup—it's better to put on fresh later
  than to *re*fresh the stuff that's been on your face for hours.

RelationTip: Choose one of your Enlist to Resist friends as your evening's Date Patrol.
Arrange for her to call you on the dot within
the first hour of your date—if things are going
lousy, it's your "I gotta go" out. If things are
great, you tell her sweetly that you'll call her
when you get home—and then, in front of
your date, tell her what time that will be.

Whatever you do—don't forget to take a last look at your look
in the mirror, smile, and relax in the knowledge that *you* did your
Dateworthy best to be your best! Remember that fun can happen
anywhere if you're with the right person . . . and if it doesn't, you
still have that Enlist to Resist phone call coming in to cancel the
experience! Hopefully, you're going someplace fun. . . .

Chapter 12

Great Dates

You know what I love about dating shows?

The producers, in an effort to make good TV, rack their brains to come up with really fun and interesting ways for a couple to interact.

Forget just meeting for coffee or a meal. They have them learn how to polka. Go to a ceramics class and make personalized mugs. Dog walking for charity. All terrific Great Date Dos. Sure, all their good intentions get shot to hell later on with the prerequisite drunken–hot-tub thing, but I think those first fifteen minutes are pure inspiration!

If you want your own Great Date Production, it's going to be up to you to do a little behind-the-scenes producing and planning to make the magic happen. (Minus the martinis and bikinis, of course, unless that's your idea of a worthy dating experience . . . if so, *get thee back to chapter 1!*)

Oh sure, in a *perfect* world, the big dating scene will go like this: Guy calls, has two exciting plans for you to choose from, and executes the details perfectly. The female lead's only responsibility is to look cute, provide fabulous conversation, sit back, and enjoy the ride.

Cut! Not as in "cut and print." As in *cut that out!*

Haven't you learned by now that anything Dateworthy—including the actual date itself—is all about what *you* put into it? You may not get perfect, but if you want a production that's at the least fun, memorable, and has the possibility of a sequel, then it's up to you to help direct this date.

So, with Oscar in mind (the award, silly, not some guy!), here are some ideas to get you pumped about your Great Date Production.

Where to Go

Oh, sure, everyone knows the rule: Whoever does the asking out should have an idea of what to do. (They are also "expected" to pay, but very often, men will insist on footing the bill or at least allow you to just leave the tip. Either way, you should be prepared with extra dough on top of your emergency twenties if you do the asking.)

Do you have a clue what you'll say when *you* make the call?

Wait . . . did you just say you *never* do the asking?

Oh, no you didn't. Because you know being Dateworthy means taking the fullest advantage of fate date moments when you may have to get the ball rolling!

So I ask again: What will you say when you make the call? And, on the what-I'm-sure-would-be-preferable flip side, what if he calls you and asks, "What would *you* like to do?"

Dating Diary

I met Bryce waiting on a particularly long line at the grocery store. He was about two people behind me, and I caught sight of him when I turned to look for other open cashiers. I finally caught his eye, rolled mine, and smiled, and we started joking about our bad luck with choosing checkout lines. I found out that Bryce had moved into the area a few weeks prior. He asked me if he could see me again and I gave him my number.

We made a date for that evening, and I decided to have him meet me at a restaurant in Greenwich Village. He was twenty minutes late and called the restaurant and asked to speak with me. "These streets make no sense!" he said. "How do I get to you?" I started to tell him about the trains and which way to walk. "I'm driving. I need driving directions." Yikes. No one drives in New York. . . .

I had no idea which streets ran which way down there to give him accurate directions. I asked the waiter who shrugged his shoulders. "Tell him to pull over and get a cab. It's easier. Besides, there's never parking down here." I got back on the phone and told Bryce this.

"Where am I supposed to put my car to get a cab?"

"In a lot?" I ventured.

He was fuming. "Forget it. Just forget it. You should've told me driving was a bad idea."

Now I was fuming. "You should've told me that you planned on driving!"

He was totally ticked off. "Look," he said. "We'll try this again some other time, okay?" and hung up . . . and never called again.

Personally, I think the ideal comeback in that instance would be: "I'll tell you what: Why don't you tell me what you were thinking, and I'll tell you what I was thinking, and we'll see which one is the favorite?" That way, you'll see whether he *really* wants to hear what you think . . . or he's just a man who didn't care enough about the date to make a plan. If he says, "I don't know . . ." you should say, "Know what? I really want you to have an idea of what you want to do to, so . . . think about it and call me back!" Click. Talk about a challenge. You didn't just throw down the gauntlet—you smacked him upside the head with it.

If it's the former—that he did have a plan, but wanted to hear your ideas—then you should be prepared to respond with an activity that includes at least some of the following:

It promotes conversation. That means, no movies or loud concerts or anything that keeps you both from talking to each other.

It's wallet-favorable. The last thing anyone needs is to blow the bank on a first date. It's unfair to whoever is paying, and, from what I've read in reader letters, it's a huge source of discomfort to women who often feel "obligated" to "pay" for their meals with sex.

It's male friendly. Unless he brings up dancing or a flower show, save that for a later date suggestion. Think in terms of activities that have to do with eating and nothing to do with him tripping or looking stupid or in any way being detrimental to the all-important male ego.

It helps you K.I.S.S. That is, helps you Keep It Short and Simple. If you have a preset time limit ("I'll meet you at four, but I really have to leave at about six"), you can exit a not-so-great date gracefully . . . and leave a great date with anticipation about the next one.

Dating Diary

... On our very first date, Charles took me to a glass-blowing studio and we made holiday ornaments.

... Mark took me to play miniature golf.

... George took me to the zoo.

... Frank took me to a kite-flying class in the park.

... David brought a thermos of hot chocolate and we watched the Macy's Thanksgiving Day Parade balloons come to life.

You might also want to consider:

+ Amusement parks. Ride the rides, go to the funhouse, share nutrient-questionable food. It's actually a great place to get him talking about his family and childhood.

+ Cooking classes. No fooling ... or drooling! Guys *love* to cook. And eat. And actually have a picture in their heads of what *you* look like in the kitchen. (He doesn't have to know it's the *last* time he'll see you in the kitchen ... just kidding.)

+ "It's not just paintings" museums. Whether it's sports or music or a chocolate exhibit, find something that you both don't have to be incredibly art-knowledgeable to enjoy. Walking around also encourages hand-holding, a bonus for him (remember, he's a two-headed being who's happy to get skin contact).

+ "Old man" sports. Bowling. Playing pool. Golf. Traditionally for old dudes, now trendy. They're games that are slow-paced with good talking downtime in between, but they're enjoyable to do and encourage fun competition.

✦ Brunch. Affordable in even five-star budget-busting restaurants, and it's early enough to . . . have another date later but not too early that you can't still get good sleep after your Saturday night date.

✦ RelationTip: Don't suggest—or accept a suggestion—unless it's something you really, truly are interested in doing. ✦

Just remember: included in your "where to go" should also be "where to meet" plans. Bottom line? If he's a fate date or someone you've been corresponding with online, tell him you'll meet him at the venue. If he's a relative or friend fix-up, a former coworker, someone from your church—anyone where there's already a built-in knowledge of each other and of each other's friends—it's okay to have him pick you up at your place, but I suggest being ready to go when he gets there so that you can get back into the public space.

And finally, make sure that you both know exactly where and when you're supposed to meet, and that you both know how to get there. If neither of you have an exact address, offer to call the restaurant for the specific information, and then offer to leave it on his machine. The last thing you want is to end up at Famous Johns on Sixth Avenue while he's waiting for you at John's Famous on Sixth Street.

Now that you have lots of Great Date Production location ideas . . . let's talk about scene spoilers.

Dating Diary

I met H.J.—a cute, New Wave singer with several huge radio and MTV hits at the time—at a popular club near my apartment. He sent a waiter over to bring me to the VIP area, where we talked and laughed for hours. Then, he asked if he could walk me home. Normally, I would never do that . . . but geez, this was H.J., and I figured just letting him walk me there but not letting him up was okay.

We held hands and kissed at the door, and he was okay with my not letting him up. When he called the next day to go out again that evening, I said yes . . . and let him up into my apartment. Unfortunately, it being a studio, the only place we could sit was the bed . . . and next thing I knew, we were making out furiously. I realized just before I got too lost in the moment that there's more than the guy you have to worry about when you invite someone up. You also have to worry about yourself—being human and totally turned on by a guy can make you compromise your rules.

Great Date Spoilers

You already know how to be Dateworthy and deal with two-headed beings. You know what to wear, what makes for great date communication, and that the dialogue and the dynamics between you two have all the makings of the start of a successful love story.

What could possibly go wrong?

Enter the Great Date Spoilers, the on-the-date irritating stuff that causes even the most promising dating scenarios to crash and burn brighter than the Dateworthy glow that should've been your close-up moment.

So, you ask, what exactly are these scene-stealing moments? The Academy recognizes the following as the top Great Date Spoilers in the Dating Production category:

Being Late. He arrives at the meeting point on time. Twenty minutes later, he's still sitting there, wondering, "Did I get the information wrong? Did I get stood up?" and then . . . just as the host informs him that he has lost his hard-to-get reservation, you show up, all apologetic and trying to be cute and charming. He is required (but resentful) to be a good sport and let it go. If he doesn't, *you* get bent out of shape that he wasn't more understanding. The mood? Irritatingly spoiled.

Being Cell-Bound. He's in the middle of a funny story when your phone rings. It's your mom, and you stay on for a while arguing about why you never call. You hang up, and he continues. Your phone rings again—this time, a business call. After a few of those, he stops trying to talk. You are angry that he's so quiet. The conversation? Spoiled and silent till he says, "Check, please."

Being Rude to Staff. When the waiter politely told you that he couldn't accommodate your special meal request, you "whatevered" him. When the guy behind the counter apologized and asked you to repeat what you said, you told him he was incompetent. Your date not only cringes—he apologizes for you (at length if he's a regular at the date place). You get highly offended and angry and say, "What, are you taking *his* side over mine?" Still embarrassed and newly ticked-off, he mutters "bitch" under his voice. You answer back, he answers back, bad things are said, and you both stomp off home. The evening? Spoiled, and so will be your reputation amongst anyone he knows.

Dating Diary

Jeremy was a gorgeous guy who was actually studying to be a chef. Every time he asked if he could cook for me—either at his place, my place, or just bring stuff for a picnic—I turned him down, mostly because, in my mind, if I was going to go on a date, I wanted to go places I normally couldn't afford to go. One night he called me and said, "It's the one-month anniversary of our first date. Why don't I come over and cook us something really special?" I said, "Better yet, why don't you save yourself all the work and let's just go to that new fusion place we just read about?" He was quiet. Then he said, "Never mind." And that was that.

Having Eating Issues. He stops at an Italian ice stand in the park—the best in the city, he says—and you refuse to get any so he has to eat alone while walking with you. Or he takes you to a restaurant that's world famous for its seafood and you order a salad, everything on the side. Or just as bad, you order several of everything, barely touch more than a modest portion, and doggy-bag the rest for later. He's either completely ticked off that you had no interest in sharing and appreciating his taste in food or wonders if you just used him for a week's worth of gourmet groceries. He'll either end up making comments or asking probing questions about your eating habits that you'll find make you uncomfortable and defensive. He'll just give up. The odds that he'll ever try to share his love of food (which is right up there with his love of sex, sports, and sleep): spoiled.

Bottom line on spoilers: Don't do them.

And don't let them be done to you.

food frights

And while we're on the subject of food—something that is linked to any date (studies show that sharing food is something that is considered very connecting and loving)—I think it's important to note that there are just some things you should never order on a first date!

> RelationTip: There's nothing wrong with having an eating preference—you're a vegetarian or are allergic to seafood—but ante up this info before he makes dinner plans.

These gastronomic disasters just waiting to happen include:

+ **Salad.** Unless it's a *chopped* salad. But most places just present these giant pieces of lettuce that you cannot possibly get your mouth around, cherry tomatoes that promise to squirt on someone, and . . . using a knife to cut it down is just way more trouble than it's worth.

+ **Linguine, spaghetti, or any other long pastas.** You can't win. You'll either slurp and flip sauce from the end of the pasta onto your blouse or your date, or roll and roll until you have a massive forkful that you have to cram into your mouth.

+ **Lobster or crab.** Wrestling with crab legs or lobster tails distracts you from the conversation at hand, and the odds of something flying off your plate and onto someone's lap are huge. Not to mention, those paper bibs look really dorky. If the restaurant doesn't give you a headstart or just take it out of the shell, avoid it.

+ **Oversized sandwiches.** It's impossible to take a bite and not look like you've got a tennis ball stuck in your cheek, or to have to make hideous mouth moves as you try to chew without opening your mouth. Also, the sandwich version of Murphy's Law—as you bite down, something will fall out from the other end—makes this a dating no-no.

+ **Garlic and onions.** That is, of course, unless *he's* also doing it.

+ **Must-floss foods.** Ribs. Corn on the cob. These are double don'ts because you have to pick them up with your hands and they are usually dripping in something.

+ **Foods you love but don't tolerate well.** Sweetie, if you know it gives you gas—save it for alone time, okay?

RelationTip: While eating, regularly take a small sip of water and gently "push" it through your teeth with your mouth closed—it will get rid of any obvious bits of food in between so that you don't have to hold back a smile during dinner conversation.

Now there's only one thing left for you to consider on your Great Date Production—how's it all going to end?

Great Date Endings

You've just had the best time.

The conversation flowed. There was lots of laughter and connecting and while, deep down, you know that this is Best Behavior Zone, you can't help but think, "Wow . . . he's terrific."

If the above is all true, then right about now, you are incredibly vulnerable to making some crucial date-ending errors. You might consider having him take you to your door. Even letting him in for a while. After all, there were no scary signposts that unnerved you. Why *not* keep the night going?

You might consider sleeping with him. Sure, you put on your old lady support stuff . . . but you figure, if you have him over, you can excuse yourself and slip into something sexier. The chemistry is unbelievable and hey, didn't he mention that he was blown away by you?

Snap out of it, woman!!!

RelationTip: Just because you spent one of the most amazing hours with someone doesn't mean you know him.

Just because the date was great doesn't mean that you should throw all of your safety and standards out the window.

If you want a second date, you've got to end the first one. You've got to tap into your self-worthfullness and find the confidence to say, "Good night," and the assertiveness to say, "I can't wait to do this again!"

Take a deep breath, look around for that Dateworthy Dude Checklist in your bag, and remember that for a man, having sex is just *sex*, not necessarily a second date. Take back your power and your sense of purpose. If you met at a public place, leave separately. If he picked you up, let him drop you off, but make it clear that a walk to the door ends at the door.

And then . . . only if you really, really like him, and you felt like the feeling was mutual, I say, go in for . . . the good-night kiss.

The effective good-night kiss is actually a tried and true technique that took me years to develop. Don't laugh! There is absolutely a way to kiss a guy that leaves him tingly and curious and wanting to kiss you again.

Allow me to share with you how to effectively do the good-night kiss.

First: Hold his hands.

Next: Say, "Thanks . . . I had the best time."

Then: Lean in and connect lips—closed mouth, slightly lingering, and then . . . a little hint of a lower-lip nibble with your lips.

Finally: Pull back, smile while holding a two-second eye-lock.

End it: Say, "I really hope we can see each other again."

It's the ultimate closer statement that lets a guy know that there's more to you than just great looks and conversation . . . but that he's going to have to keep coming back if he wants to see what that is.

Now, I knew you were going to ask. . . . *Yes,* the good-night kiss is still effective after brunch or lunch or early-in-the-day dates. It's called the good-night kiss because, done correctly, it will inspire Reaction Central for the rest of his night. And that's good. Leaving him with Reaction Central in full control of his dreams is definitely a way to burn you into Gray Matter Headquarters!

As the director of this dating epic . . . can't you just picture that great good-night kiss moment?

SCENE: The leading lady shuts the door/leaves the restaurant/pool hall. The leading man watches her, a small grin on his face and he thinks about what they'll do the next time they see each other. . . .

Oh, wait. Cut. Don't print that. I see a revision coming up. . . .

He watches her, a small grin on his face, and, in a voiceover, we hear what he's thinking: "That was a nice kiss, but . . . I don't think I'll see her again."

Yup. That was a wrap. Talk about a lousy ending.

The date we thought was great . . . but who disappears, never to be seen or heard from again. And you'll wonder, what happened? I thought I did everything perfectly. *What went wrong?*

My answer: Maybe you did everything perfectly—but perhaps it was just the wrong audience. Or the wrong timing.

I'm betting that if you feel confident about the date, most likely it *was* him . . . *not* you.

He Just Wasn't In To You!

Now for some top-secret information that most books won't—or can't—tell you. Because I have so many male readers, I'm able to get a sense of why guys don't call. The reasons are so incredibly simple and straightforward . . . and if more women knew them, they would probably stop beating themselves up with an ice-cream spoon and just do as a man does: chalk it up to a loss and move forward, with renewed determination to win the next one.

Here are the top "it's *really* not you" reasons your date went bust:

+ **Timing.** Women may get serious when they meet the right guy, but men . . . men get serious with whomever they are dating at the right time in their lives. If they meet you at that "I'm still a studly single" moment, and you're unbelievably Dateworthy—the kind that they would *want* to get serious with—they move on to what they really need at the moment: the "wild sex" girl.

+ **Temp-ex.** He was with a girl he loved for a while, but he came up several carats short when she gave him the fabulous-finger-hardware ultimatum. He then starts to date with no intention of

Dating Diary

When I told Rob that I loved roller coasters, he took me to a Six Flags park for our first date. We rode everything, shared park junk food on benches, and talked and talked. We were surprised at how many "me too!" moments we had, and how weird it was that we both had been at two of the same music events several months before but never bumped into each other. "I guess it's all timing," he said. "You meet someone when you're supposed to meet them."

The afternoon date extended into the evening, where we rode rides in the dark and held hands and hugged a lot. By the time he drove me home, I was exhausted but extremely happy. He walked me to the door, I gave him the good-night kiss, and he grabbed my hand as I turned and said, "I can't wait to see you again."

Well, I guess he could wait . . . and wait . . . and wait. I broke down and called . . . and called . . . and finally, one day I caught him on the phone. I tried that cheery "I was just wondering if you were okay because I didn't hear from you" thing, but when all I got was, "No, I'm okay." I flipped.

"So why haven't you called me? What did I do wrong?"

"Nothing, no reason."

"Oh, come on. . . . We had the best time, right? Don't you think you owe me an explanation?"

"Remember what I said about timing? Well . . . I guess you were the right girl but at the wrong time because my ex and I decided to give us another shot."

"Oh . . . oh, okay." And then I wanted to kick myself as these "reassure me, please" words came out: "So, it wasn't me?"

"No," he said. "You're great. It's me."

doing anything but having the greatest time he can have to forget her—and he doesn't. So he goes back and leaves you hanging.

✦ **Wrong audience.** He had the best time with you, but he feels about as attracted as he does to one of his buddies. Have you ever said, "He's such a great guy, but he's just not *my* great guy"? So has he. About great girls. About *you*.

Feel better? You should!

Because, remember, you are playing a numbers game . . . and this guy just left you free to pursue your spare "Satur-date"!

Just know this—the more Great Date Productions you work on, the easier it will be for you to get the players and the chemistry right.

The important thing for you to do is do what I did: Chalk up the really bad ones to funny girls-night-out stories, and keep plunging right back in with all the things I learned from experience!

✦ RelationTip: Women who are asked out on second dates say that they were less concerned about impressing him and more concerned about having a great time.

If you're left with the question that's on many women's minds: What if my last dating story wasn't so funny? And my "really bad one" was just that—*really bad* and super-painful? How do I find a way to take the plunge back into dating? So many questions . . . so many answers to those issues . . . in the next chapter.

Chapter 13

Dating after Destruction

Whenever I get a letter from a reader who just went through a nasty breakup or, even worse, was put through such incredible emotional or physical abuse by a man who told her that he loved her, I often end my response with, "I want you to wrap your arms around yourself and squeeze and know that I just sent you that great, big hug."

Sure, being hugged by yourself and imagining someone else doing it is not the same as having someone who truly loves you there and doing it for you. But I've done it at times of terrible hurt and heartbreak, and I always feel better. I think that if you go with the idea of giving yourself a big hug sent by someone with you in mind, heart, and spirit, you still believe that others can care for you like that. I also think that you find your ability to make yourself feel better, even for a moment.

Those two things—the ability to believe and the ability to be strong for a moment if it means making things better—are really good signs that you will find that courage to give dating, and all the emotional stuff that goes with it, another shot.

The Breakup Breakdown

In chapter 2, I talked about how you need to go through several stages of grieving before you are ready to jump into the dating pool. But before you can even go through *that* process—which is dealing with self-healing and growth—you need to go through several stages to strip yourself of the relationship itself:

+ Knowing that it's really over

+ Breaking apart

+ Stabilizing

+ Starting over

Each one just . . . am I allowed to say . . . *sucks*? (I guess I just did.)

Know It's Really Over

I know it seemed so shocking at the time, but . . . I'm betting if you look back on the relationship, there were lots of arguments and disagreements and dissatisfaction and, man, even the sound of the way he brushed his teeth would cause you to grit yours.

I'm sure that it all was so routine—"just the way we are, I guess"—that you never, ever thought someone would have enough and end it. But the tension increased and then . . . he walked.

Dating Diary

When I caught Frank cheating and lying, I offered to give him another chance if he ended it. He chose not to and told me that I was free to stay or go—he didn't care.

I stopped eating, sleeping . . . I cried every day, and the pain in the gut area was just so unbelievable that I never, ever thought I could survive it. My friends and family were so worried about my health, and I couldn't blame them—I didn't recognize the person I saw in the mirror, nearly twenty-five pounds thinner and with giant circles under her eyes. I prepared to move out—looking at apartments on my own after work, commuting back home two hours, and then watching . . . at this point, numbly . . . while he whistled and primped and got ready to meet his girl.

"Bye," he'd say. And sometimes he didn't come back in the mornings. But I kept thinking it was a phase, that he'd go for counseling, that . . .

I finally gave up and moved out. Well, he moved me. He got the U-Haul and packed my stuff and helped me out of his home and into mine. And when he brought all the boxes in, he looked around and smiled, and said, "Hey, you know, this isn't a bad place. It's actually pretty nice." I looked at him incredulously. "Okay, gotta go—can I get a hug?"

As he walked toward me with his arms outstretched, I finally got angry. "Get out of my house," I said, very quietly and controlled. And feeling in control for the first time since this started. And he did.

RelationTip: Most relationships don't end just out of the blue—someone was experiencing the blues long before.

If you two have that kind of dramatic, highly volatile relationship thing going on, it's sometimes hard to know whether this is just a temporary thing . . . or if it's really the big one. But certainly, the fat lady, if you will, has sung your last love note if:

+ One partner wants to be free.

+ Your partner has done something so heinous that you absolutely cannot forgive him.

+ You both agree that you're just too tired and/or battered to even consider that there's anything left to salvage.

RelationTip: While it takes two people to make a relationship work, it only takes one person to end it.

Know it's really over when one of you is no longer willing to be in it—when that person says it, and then follows up with avoidance and then with . . . dating other people. I don't think it gets any more painful than the moment you witness that.

Breaking Apart

You knew it was over, but watching your man actually leave and start his own life and leave you behind . . . well, you think, *that just can't be happening.*

But it is . . . and as hurt as you were in the last stage, this one is

Dating Diary

I knew that Frank continued to see the woman he had cheated on me with, but I didn't know her and never expected to actually run into them. I went into a bar to meet a friend one night, and there they were, on stools, wrapped around each other. I just stopped and stared. My friend tried to hustle me out of the place, but I couldn't budge. It's like trying not to look at a bad accident on the side of the road . . . you just can't help yourself. They saw me and he said something to her like, "Let's leave."

I walked up to him. "That is why we broke up? You left me for that ugly little thing?" I felt like such a loser but I couldn't stop myself. He just left. I went to the parking lot and cried. The worst part? She was his mom's hairdresser, and despite the fact that his mom knew everything that was going on . . . she continued to have her hair done by her.

Ugly, right? I know. I'll chalk up that unattractive moment to just being incredibly, deeply wounded.

going to be a mixed bag of anger, fear, confusion, and even panic. You're thinking: "He's really gone. What will I do? How dare he? What happens now? I can't even imagine ever going through this again."

It's even worse if you two had one time exchanged vows before family and friends and promised happily-ever-after. You feel so incredibly betrayed and like you're *used up*. "I don't want to be a 'divorcée,'" you think. Add to the mix that you have kids . . . and now, you feel like you cannot allow yourself to feel anything to help maintain their sense of security.

Actually, right now is the most important time for you to deal with those feelings, to get them out. Remember when I said, "Grief shared is grief diminished"? You've got to talk to trusted friends, relatives, clergy, even a professional to help you understand that this is not the end of your life—just the end of *this* relationship, one relationship of many that you currently share . . . and will eventually share in the future.

Stabilizing

Eventually, the anger and the hurt and the histrionics just get too much to keep doing on a day-to-day level (that only happens in the world of soap operas where they get paid really well to endure that level of emotional drainage). So you shift and adjust. Allow yourself to enjoy things again. Find that there are hours in a day that go by when you did not have a thought process of him . . . and kick yourself for having to think about how long you didn't think about him.

Once you're here, you can start looking into doing the grieving work for the old relationship as mentioned in chapter 2. It's important to actually work through each step in order—jumping ahead to get through the healing process faster can't work if your emotions aren't in the right place for the particular exercise.

I know you're hurting, so I'm going to save you having to flip back:

Denial: You still think there's a shot at getting back together despite the fact that he's kept his distance . . . and that your relationship wasn't as good as you try to remember it.

Depression: You realize that it's truly over and feel unattractive, unneeded . . . unworthy of love (this is totally one of those

Dating Diary

*After I moved out of Frank's, I immersed myself in work and seeing friends.
I pitched the idea of a romance column that's still in YM to this day. I went
out with friends and flirted furiously with guys just to see them react to me.
I'd sometimes take or give out numbers, but kept dates at arm's length.
When I met a guy who was kind and thoughtful and caring—he could be
something, I thought—I stopped those thoughts dead in their tracks because I did not trust my judgment. My goodness, all the guys I rejected
until Frank, and I was so sure that with him it was real love. How could I
know that I wouldn't pick another dud next time?*

"wrap your arms around you and give yourself a big hug from
me" times).

Anger: From "How *dare* he?" to "How do I not let another jerk
in my life?" Angry energy turned around in a positive way can be
very proactive and healing.

Acceptance: It's done. And you can't change that . . . but you
can learn from that and turn it into some Good Luggage.

This can be a really tough time and the temptation to do something bad—numb the pain by drugging, drinking, or binge eating;
hiding out from work, school, family, friends, or church; or even
taking part in meaningless one-night stands with the ex just to feel
loved—is a very common reaction.

Before you even think about venturing into that territory, I want
you to stop and remember: In order to find self-worth*full*ness, you
have to fill your life *full* of positive things. Did Tina Turner allow

Ike to turn her into a drunken old has-been? Make like Proud Mary and keep on rollin' forward.

Starting Over

You've reached the point where you know your life does not depend on this past relationship. In other words: Hot *damn*, you got through it! Time to move forward.

But before you can start fresh, you've got to forgive.

No, you don't have to forgive that idiot that left you. Okay, if you've got kids, it would be nice if you could find a way to forge a friendship with the man, but you don't have to do it immediately—and definitely *not* before you take care of yourself.

Forgive yourself for the fact that you didn't make a good choice. And forgive him for getting in your path to make that choice.

Forgive yourself for any dumb things you did while you were trying to keep it together. Oh, and for those really juicy, God-awful revenge dreams you had.

Forgive yourself for all the mistakes you will make as you start over. Congratulate yourself that you're willing to try.

And finally, trust yourself that this time, you'll take your time and make a better choice.

Yesss! Big hugs all around!

Dating after Death

Being a cancer survivor, I've been around many women who have lost a spouse and had to get back into the dating market again.

Many of them had a hard time with the idea. Some because they felt "guilty," particularly because his family made her feel like he wouldn't approve, or that they felt she hadn't been "grieving" long enough. Others hated the idea of telling a potential date "my hus-band died" and then, of course, having to answer questions about what happened, opening old wounds. And many . . . frankly, they felt that he *was* the love of their lives, that they would've been to-gether forever, and that they do not believe that anything could ever match that again . . . so why try?

RelationTip: We do not get just one great love in our lives. As our lives change and grow, so will what we need from another person.

I say try because the man you loved so dearly would want you to be happy. I say go for it because the death of your husband or partner changed you just enough that yes, it's possible that there's another man out there who is *now* a perfect love for you.

So please . . .

First, follow the grieving process as outlined starting on page 24, and don't skip the anger part. As a matter of fact, anger is such a natural process to go through after someone so deeply loved dies, essentially leaving you to start over.

Second, don't apologize to anyone for stepping back into the dating scene. If you feel you've gone through the grieving process and you're ready to explore, that's entirely personal and up to you. I know one young mom who was criticized for going on her first date only three months after her husband died of cancer. This was a woman who had to nurse a young, dying man around the clock for more than a year, and who had started her grieving process be-fore the actual passing. If someone criticizes you, say, "I appreciate your concern, but until you've walked in my shoes, I don't think you're qualified to know what's best for me."

Third, don't feel like you have to detail your husband's death on every date. If a guy asks if you were ever married, simply say, "Yes, but that ended some time ago, and it's one of those long stories that I'll save for another time." If he's a good one, he won't push the issue any further.

Fourth, there is no such thing as *the soul mate*, the one and only person that was destined to be with you. It's a total *fractured fairy tale* and a term used by people who feel they need to prove just how *deep* their love is. There are lots of guys out there whom you haven't met but will stir your soul, and your heart. You just have to keep dating until you connect with them.

Give yourself a chance on this. Everyone I've seen move on has been surprised at how much love they actually still had to offer.

And speaking of fractured fairy tales . . . in the next chapter, we'll look at those lamentable legends of what love is supposed to be, break them down, and rebuild them into a more truthful tale.

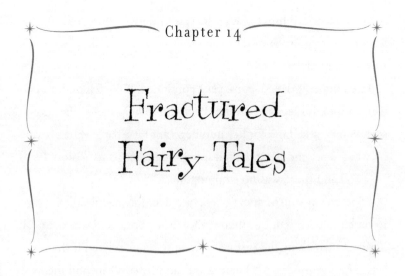

Chapter 14

Fractured Fairy Tales

So, I was sitting there in some kind of bright blue satin dress with a giant white bow that was expertly sewn in that area right where your behind is at its biggest. "Oh, it's a Tiffany box theme!" said my friend, who was getting married to a man she referred to as her soul mate, but whom I simply referred to as Squinty (she felt his glasses made him look "too nerdy" and made him get contact lenses a few weeks before the wedding). And as I stood near the ice sculpture and listened for the umpteenth time to the ever-more-romantic myth about how they met and fell in love ("It was at *first sight*. They both knew within the first *ten* minutes that they would be together *forever!*"), I struggled not to interject a little bit of reality. Suddenly, I could hold back no more.

"When they met . . ." I said, tugging uncomfortably at the bow that had now shifted and was giving me a wedgie. "When they met, she barely noticed him because she was so wasted you could add the legal limits from twenty states and still not come close to what she had consumed."

I heard the horrified gasps, yet I continued. "She fell on him and threw up on his leg. He was kind enough to help me get her home and then he asked me for her number. Not for a date—but because he wanted to send her a dry-cleaning bill for his pants." Now I was on a roll and there was no stopping me.

"She got in touch, apologized, and asked if she could take him to lunch. He agreed, but then it took him about two weeks to call her back, which he did primarily because he wondered if she came across his eyeglass case." There was dead silence all around me now and I closed in for the kill.

"That phone conversation was actually fun, and they got together again, became friends, and then, bored one night, they ended up in the sack, where they finally found something they both enjoyed doing together." Boom! Down went Grandma. "And then, my dear wedding-goers, he popped the question only after she gave him an ultimatum!" Triumphant, I turned to make a dramatic departure . . . and the bow caught fire.

"*Ohmigod*, Dennie! Your *butt* is on fire!" The moment the water hit my back (turning the lower part of the dress completely transparent), I was out of my tell-it-like-it–is daydream and back to being a bridesmaid at what everyone referred to as Barbie's Dream Wedding.

That fractured fairy tale has never been told—that is, until now, because it's been twelve years and, like Barbie and Ken, these two have since gone their separate ways. And while I can't remember much about that day beyond the blue and the bow and my burning butt, I *do* completely recall the way the other, always-a-bridesmaid, single, catch-the-bouquet girls looked when they heard the fractured fairy tale just before it was trashed by my get-real scenario. They *believed* that this was how it would happen to them.

Why do I feel completely obligated to dispel those awful fractured fairy tales people perpetuate to make others feel that theirs is a story that Disney would do well to animate? Because I *hate* that so many women will compare their perfectly good, hard-earned, Dateworthy relationships to those stupid ideals and then feel that their story just will *never* bear repeating. Do you know how many girlfriends I have who have met someone on a—*horrors!*—dating site, and tell me, "If this works out, we're going to make up a better story for the kids!"?

> RelationTip: When you feel like you constantly have to embellish how amazing your relationship is, most likely it ain't.

The Fractured Fairy Tales

Let's take a walk through Dennie's Magic Kingdom, where Red Riding Hood carries pepper spray to go into the woods, Cinderella would've claimed her own damn shoe the next day, and fractured fairy tales are given a reality check.

The Soul Mate

He is the man who is your destiny, who was your lover in past lives, and you two were *meant* to be.

Oh, puh-*leeze*! Are you *kidding* me? What if you met this so-called "soul mate" when you were in the tenth grade? And you broke up after college? Now what? Are you saying that anyone after that will always be *lesser* than? Or will you do what countless other women do: "I *thought* he was my soul mate, but I was wrong. If he was, we'd still be together. *This* one . . . now *he's* truly my soul mate." Talk about changing the rules as you go along!

By allowing yourself to believe that there is someone who is your destiny, you don't actively work on keeping the relationship alive and healthy. Also, you may end up being trapped in a relationship that is truly not working, *just* because—in believing that he is "the only one" who will ever make you feel this way—you refuse to let this go.

Personally, I think that people who look for a "soul mate" are people who are looking for a person who makes them *feel*. They don't have passion or excitement in their own lives, and they are looking for someone to give them that. To them, feeling that *alive* is worth overlooking all the other things that the person they are with is lacking.

Fixing the Fracture: Look for someone who enhances your life, not gives life to it. We have so many layers and facets to our personalities—believe that there is more than one or two, or two hundred, men out there who can add brilliance to them.

Love at First Sight

That's it. You saw each other across the room and your eyes locked. You started talking to each other and within five minutes, you just couldn't imagine ever spending another second without him. Actually, it's kind of "soul mate lite"—all of the bullshit, but only a third of the mystical "we knew each other in another life" factor.

Lots of women are First Sighters—that is, if they don't feel that instant attraction within the first few minutes of meeting, they dismiss the guy as someone they have no "chemistry" with. Sigh.

Dating Diary

I was walking out of a club one night after being ditched by my boyfriend-of-the-moment (who, I later found out, got drunk and forgot he was on a date and took another girl home). That's when Jon stopped me. Just a little taller than me, buff body, and a face that went way beyond movie-star cute, he let go of my arm and stared directly into my eyes. "I'm sorry, I didn't mean to grab you like that. It's just . . . I'm sorry, but I'm completely taken by you."

"I was just leaving. . . ." I said.

"No, wait. I know you don't have to stay and you probably have a boyfriend you're going home to, but . . . my name is Jon and I'm a part-owner of this club and I'd love it if you would just hang out a little bit." I did. And did again, night after night. And we got close, fast. This divorced dad of two kept telling me how "connected" he was to me, that I was his "soul mate."

"You are someone," he said, "who I think I always knew existed but never thought I'd meet and so I married the wrong person." I loved the attention, but after a while I realized that I didn't love the man the way he did me, and it got to be too much. One afternoon, Jon told me that his ex was going to drop off the girls early and asked if I minded leaving right after brunch. Just as I was heading out, the doorbell rang. As he opened it . . . there was a mirror image of me. And two mini-mes—twin 5-year-olds who absolutely could've been my daughters. The ex stared at me, shocked at the "recognition."

Too weird. I ended things that day.

Do you realize that "chemistry" without taking the time to learn what ingredients you're mixing can be highly combustible and blow up in your face?

The biggest problem with believing in love at first sight is that you pass over some incredibly Dateworthy guys in favor of a fleeting feeling of pure attraction and lust. People who are First Sighters are often in love with the idea of love—they watch all the first-sight movies, read all the romance novels . . . they go with that intense feeling because they just think that love *should* feel that way.

Fixing the Fracture: Love takes time to grow and should be based on respect, love, honesty, caring, thoughtfulness . . . all those Non-Negotiables I've been blah-blah-blahing about! Give a guy more than just a few minutes—or even a few dates—to get to know him. Don't allow some magical, invisible Cupid's arrow moment to be responsible for whom you date. Take charge and responsibility for building true love.

Opposites Attract

He's mild, you're jalapeño hot wings. He's a *Three Stooges* guy, you're still bemoaning the end of *Friends*. You believe that it's what makes you so different that keeps things interesting, and you always go for the guy that leaves your friends going, "Huh??" Fascinating concept, except . . . how come you have yet to find one of these opposites you actually want to stay with?

Listen. The key word in this dating urban legend is that it's about attraction. I n totally see how someone so not like you may attract nning—even motivate you to try something you u would, like, I don't know, exploring the music or bungee jumping. If the only thing opposites

195

Dating Diary

*Andy was a summer love, and when he was leaving to go back to his real
life several thousand miles away, we vowed to keep it together. Within two
weeks, I was bored out of my mind. I loved getting the nightly "tuck you
in" phone calls and the cards and letters just as much as I loved finding
creative ways to tell him how crazy I was about him . . . but soon I was secretly dating up a storm.*

*Still I kept up the pretense of this mad, long-distance love thing and fig-
ured that if I ever saw him again, we'd just have another intense fling till
he left. Needless to say, my correspondence—and his longing—caused
him to fly back and announce that he was leaving his job and moving here
to be together. Whoa. I was soooo not thrilled, and he saw it. As a matter
of fact, seeing him was such a shock. I had had his face so Johnny
Depp–fantasy-morphed, I . . . I don't know. Anyway, it was a complete
and total disaster. He had brought a bag to stay over, and I told him he
couldn't but offered to pay for his hotel and apologized. He left and I
never heard from him again. (Sorry, by the way, wherever you are. . . .)*

share *is* attraction, however, not a real heart-and-soul connection,
then the opposites are doomed.

People who consciously choose opposites over and over again are
often Drama Queens. They want drama, not a real relationship that
they have to actually put time and thought into. They have a huge
fear that they are not that interesting . . . and they look for someone
so they can be "interesting by association."

Fixing the Fracture: There's nothing wrong with keeping yourself open to meeting different types of guys. As long as you two share the same values and goals—and what's most obvious to your friends is how compatible you are and how terrific your relationship is—strictly-Gap guy meets Goth girl is a winner.

Absence Makes the Heart Grow Fonder

If he can't have you whenever he wants you, he'll be hooked. And when you do see him, he'll appreciate you more, and this will drive him to pop the question so that he doesn't have to be without you ever again. Hmmm . . . so . . . how are you going to sustain *that* when you two are married and living in a studio apartment? Hide under the bed for hours? Crash at a friend's house until you're sure he's frantic to see you again? Have you ever heard of "out of sight, *out of mind?*"

Can you hear me now? Long-distance relationships are hard to maintain, despite the fact that the world has all kinds of ways to reach out and touch. That's actually kind of deceiving . . . you can reach out, but you certainly can't touch, or hug, or kiss the person you care about. And he doesn't get to smell your skin or run his fingers through your hair or feel any kind of connection—*this* you would decide to do to a two-headed being who *values* the physical connection over communication?

Needless to say, a person who doesn't mind being apart from someone isn't really invested in that someone. Choosing the hard-to-get-to doesn't read as hard-to-get—it comes off as hard-of-heart.

Fixing the Fracture: If you care about someone, you'll want to spend quality time being near each other. Be honest with yourself: Are you choosing out-of-area relationships just because you've been burned before, and this feels safer—and something you feel more in control of? If so, then perhaps you need to take a step back from dating and deal with your closeness issues.

$\mathcal{B}eing$ "In $\mathcal{L}ove$" Is $\mathcal{P}referable$ to $Just$ $\mathcal{L}oving$ $Someone$

You are both having the best time. You get along great. He's got the Non-Negotiable goods and treats you accordingly. You are just sooo in love with him and life and every new thing that you two discover. And then . . . what's this? He's still great, but . . . where's the passion, that new-sneaker feeling (you know what I mean—that sudden, springy, I-bet-I-can-jump-higher-than-an-NBA-All-Star charge), the *rush*? You're over it because while you do love him, you've realized you're just not "in love" anymore. Ugh. Could that be any more *damaging*?

People who need to be "in love" are often people who grew up with parents who divorced and were told, "Yes, I love your father, but I'm not 'in love' with him anymore." Getting that message early on—that "in love" was what kept people together—can often color the way a person views how a relationship is supposed to work. They are also people who have never been in a relationship long enough to understand that real love isn't like it is in the movies: It doesn't just happen; it does take work.

Fixing the Fracture: The sign of a really good relationship *is* that comfortable, "you are my family" kind of feeling. It's knowing that this guy's got your back, that he'll be there for you, that (although this scenario may not be all that exciting), he'll get up in the middle of the night and find a twenty-four-hour drugstore if it means relieving your chronic cough. If you have all this but find yourself in an "I need to be giddy" rut, you can spice things up by having date nights, buying sexy board games, surprising him at the office with nothing on but a trench coat (obviously, this works better if he doesn't work in a cubicle). . . . Choosing love or "in love"—reserve that for shoe shopping.

And finally, my favorite fractured fairy tale of all time:

It's Better to Settle Than to Be Alone

You feel like you've been dating *forever*, and you still haven't found a Dateworthy guy who finds you Dateworthy as well. You figure, the only thing getting younger is the competition so . . . you take out your Dateworthy Dude Checklist and start crossing off things. You start negotiating on those Non-Negotiables. Hey, no one's perfect . . . but life would seem that way if you could at least have someone to be with.

I'm sorry. Can you hold on a second? I just need a moment to bang my head against the wall.

Forget that. Let's get right into this. *You do not need a man to complete you!* My Portuguese-wisdom-spouting mother told me a long time ago that she "did not bring half a person into this world," and it seems to me that too many women don't realize that they don't have to be someone's "better half" to make their lives better.

If being with a man means compromising all the things that you hold dear, feeling a pit instead of butterflies at the thought of seeing him, not being happy, but settling for "at least I don't have to keep dating anymore" contentment . . . then that is just so damn *undateworthy* of you.

Don't settle because you are scared or not having any luck with the guys you've dated. Instead, go back and work on building yourself up again. And keep *trying*. If there's one thing you can learn from my dating stories: Most people don't get it right the first, oh, I don't know, I'd say one-hundred-and-seventy-six times. But then . . . aha! You like yourself enough to take yourself out one day for a manicure, and you stop at a post office to pick up some stamps, and while you're waiting in line the guy behind you comments on your floral choice, and he's cute and when you leave, he chases you down the street clutching a daisy he just bought from a corner deli and asks you for your number.

It happened to me. Right after several stand-ups, put-downs, scary signposts, and one moron who kept calling me the wrong name all night.

Fixing the Fracture: Don't settle for someone just to keep from being alone. And don't settle for being alone either. Just don't settle.

And They Lived Happily Ever After

Actually, have you seen what the divorce rate is? Around half of all marriages fail. However, it is a myth worth hoping for.

✳

Okay. Now before you nod off and dream about you and one of *People* magazine's Sexiest Man Alive men, I want you to hold up your engagement ring finger and repeat after me:

I swear not to perpetuate any of the above myths.
To tell other women just how much work they have to
put into being Dateworthy, and finding Dateworthy,
and keeping things relationship-worthy.
Upon receiving fabulous ring-finger hardware, I will take
a pass on fractured fairy tales and instead, pass on my copy of
Dateworthy to a friend so that she too will know she has
the power to get the relationship she wants.

Now that I have you in the mood to swear by something, let's forge ahead to the Ten First Date Commandments.

Chapter 15

The Ten First Date Commandments

As they say on those mall maps: YOU ARE HERE.

Hopefully, it was by way of the scenic route, and you enjoyed the ride to Dateworthiness.

Or . . . perhaps you did what I always do. And that's skip right to the at-a-glance, troubleshooting guide because I'm in a hurry and just need some kind of "how do I get this to work *now*?" basics and *then* I'll go back when I have some time and get into learning all the other cool features.

Caught you, didn't I?

It's absolutely understandable if you literally *just* bought this book and your date is in three hours. Actually, I'm *impressed* if that's the case—looking for a little basic training just before you hit the dating trenches is a completely Dateworthy instinct.

It's totally unacceptable otherwise. Looking for the quick fix, miracle cure when it comes to being Dateworthy, to acquire the skills and knowledge to feel self-worthfull enough to call the shots and not feel like you are at the mercy of some mystical dating force . . . that takes time. And effort. And yes, even a little bit of prep work.

Aren't you *worth* that little extra time?

That said, I guess it's okay for those of you who have that pending date to take just a little peek at what's in store for you before you go back and begin your true Dateworthy journey later. And for those of you who are here via the scenic route—welcome to the wrap party!

After all, isn't it the sample at the fragrance counter that inspires you to invest in the full size? (Oh, come on, that was a really good analogy—you totally knew what I meant.)

So . . . let me let you go ahead and take a look at my Ten First Date Commandments.

No. 1. Never, Ever Have Sex

Having sex on a first date doesn't make you a bad person. It does, however, compromise your ability to:

+ Stay detached to really scrutinize the guy you're dating.

+ Stay safe—after all, unless you're going to do it in a public bathroom, having sex means having to go somewhere and be alone with someone you barely know.

+ Weed out the hit-it-and-run guys.

+ Not feel that your actions were to blame for him not calling.

Yes, guys are two-headed beings and will push for sex. However, if he's a guy who's interested in who *you* are, he's not actually expecting to get it. (As a matter of fact, studies show that most guys stick around if they *don't* have sex.) Remember: Sex should be the perk of a good relationship, not a first-date party favor. So put on that ugly support bra and granny hose and get going!

RelationTip: Sex may sell—but first-date sex sells you short.

No. 2. K.I.S.S. *(Keep It Short & Simple)*

The last thing anyone wants to do is be stuck in a date that feels like an advanced calculus class with no end to the period in sight. Trust me: You may feel funny saying, "I'd love to meet you—say around 5:00?—but I've got to be somewhere at 7 tonight," but having that advance plan is a whole lot kinder than trying to find a way to bolt in the middle of a date with a nice guy who just isn't for you. (If he's a jerk, kindness rules are fair game to be broken.)

Set a time limit and have a girlfriend call you near the time you are "supposed" to leave. If it's a good date, you can say, "Oh, I *don't* have to go and help out? Great—I'll talk to you later." And—if *he's* not already scheduled—you have the option of extending your time together.

No. 3. Be a Good Listener

There's nothing that a two-headed being likes as much as sex, as having someone ask questions and show an intense interest in what he has to say. (I'll be honest: Those first few dates in the Best Behavior Zone are probably the most you'll *ever* see him talk, so def-

Dating Diary

Dean was a personal ad date who sounded fun on the phone, so we met for dinner. As soon as I got there, he said to me, "Oh . . . wow . . . your picture looked a lot more model-like." I tried to joke through the awkward moment.

"Wow, thanks. Sorry that you didn't read my 5'3" reference in my letter!" He wouldn't let it go.

"No, really, I just figured you were taller. And I guess more in proportion for your height." I was fuming—this less-than-tall idiot making me feel less than . . . but . . . I was also hungry. So I continued on.

We sat down and I looked at the menu and saw that they had a "signature" shrimp cocktail with shrimp that had to be flown in first-class from some place from the Florida Keys—and it was incredibly expensive. Yum. I ordered eight of them.

Oh, yes I did. That was thirty-two shrimp and over $70. He was mortified.

"I guess you like shrimp," he offered. "But do you really think you need thirty-two?" I sure did. And I let him talk, and I ate to the point of busting and then said, "I feel sick. I think I ate too many shrimp. Excuse me." I went toward the bathroom . . . and out the door . . . and never, ever felt bad about it. Definitely a good shrimp/bad shrimp night.

initely encourage the chatter!) As you know, a conversation should be like a tennis game, with two people lobbing back and forth. But your goal here is to get the info on *him*, not to hear the stories you already know, so be sure to always find a way to follow your response with an inquiry that gets the ball back into his court. By appearing to be a good listener to him—and by actually really listening and getting to know if he's got partner potential—you both score: He's flattered, you're informed!

No. 4. Don't Trash-Talk Your Ex

Just as there should never be any X-rated conversation, there should never be ex-saturated conversation in a first-date situation. Sure, you will both be curious—and rightly so—about how long it's been since a breakup, but going on and on about what a jerk, or a mistake, or a waste of time someone was will only make a guy feel:

+ **Uneasy.** Will you be trash-talking *him* this way one day? Or worse, unable to let go and, perhaps, turn stalker on him?

+ **Bored.** He'd rather be talking about himself than some other guy.

+ **Turned off.** Why did you allow yourself to stay with someone that bad?

+ **Rebound-cautious.** No one gets *that* caught up in a past relationship unless it's not truly history!

RelationTip: There's a fine line between love and hate, and for guys . . . well, passionate hate reads, "I'm still not over that X-man."

No. 5. Don't Be an Open Book

Your date is not your therapist. Nor is he your priest or your hairdresser. (Why is it that every woman I know, myself included, feels the need to spill life secrets the moment we're in the "hair chair"?

Dating Diary

Angelo was really depressed about his dead-end job, but he wasn't sure what he'd want to do next. Actually, if he hadn't busted out his knee playing high-school ball, he may have had a career. But it didn't matter, anyway, because his parents were really pushing him into accounting, so he went to school for it and got a degree, which took him a lot longer than he expected because he had to drop out for a little while to go into rehab . . . which, thank God, he never had to deal with again because now he's totally against anything that is mind-altering and thinks everyone needs to treat his body like a temple. Actually, maybe the job wouldn't be so bad if it weren't for his cubicle-mate with this habit of clearing his throat all the time. . . .

Why do you need to know all this about Angelo? As I sat on this interminable date (that's right, folks—he was so darn sexy I forgot to plan a time-limit call), I wondered the same thing.

Do we think that perhaps if our stylist knew everything, he'd actually give us a better haircut? One that was bouncin' and behavin' a whole lot better than our lives were going? Oh, the stories my stylist could tell!)

The object of a first date is to give—and get—a good impression. You know how you should always stay alert to what's going on by avoiding alcohol on a first date? Skip the wine—*and* the whine—if you want to make this date a successful, informative one.

Don't go on and on about all the rotten stuff going on with you.

Why would he want to get involved in your life if *you* don't even like being there? *Do* tell him the things about you that you think make you look your best—just don't forget to take time to find out the same from him. And while we're talking about discreet disclosure, let's not forget another open book liability: Being too open about where you work or live can compromise your safety if this guy turns out to be a creep.

RelationTip: If you want to be a must-read, don't offer up <u>Cliffs Notes</u>.

No. 6. Don't Bring Up the "M" Word

Bringing up marriage on a first date is truly enough to make a man break out into hives. And the man who doesn't . . . is truly a man who should make *you* break into a run.

Talking about marriage may mean that you fall into the most-bound-to-be-broken-up-with behavior type of woman I call the Time Bomb. It makes you sound desperate, and makes the guy desperately worried about asking you on a second date for fear that you may view it as a commitment from him.

And if *he* brings it up? Be as wary as a guy would be of you. This is a guy who is either a) saying things that he thinks will make him come off as Mr. Commitment Guy to get into your pants, or b) a First Sighter—someone who falls in love with your Best Behavior Zone and just when you succumb, backs off and says, "This is moving too fast." You can always brush him off with your own "M" word: "*Maybe* someday . . . when I've taken the time to find the right guy."

No. 7. Dare to Have Spares

Know that old wives' tale about putting your eggs in one basket? Girl, they may be old—but they *are* wives . . . meaning, at one point or another, they nabbed that man!

As I've said before, dating is a numbers game: The more men you date, the better the odds are of meeting some really good eggs. But to increase your chances of seeing—and being seen—by a Dateworthy guy, you've got to have a dating rotation. Everyone is in the Best Behavior Zone those first three months. By not concentrating on just one guy for that amount of time—and having at least one or two spares—it won't feel so much like wasted time when one of them ends up being less than Dateworthy.

Just be honest. Never tell someone he is your only one when he's really just your number one . . . of several.

No. 8. Trust Your Instincts

Hmmm. . . . He's not exhibiting any scary signposts or giving off cautionary clues that you need to file away for future observance. He seems cool and attentive, funny and interesting, and yet . . . you can't put your finger on it, but something about this guy makes you uneasy.

Crime stats show that many women are the victims of a crime—like date rape—because they ignored, or brushed away, a gut feeling that something just wasn't right . . . especially if the guy seemed to be everything they wanted in a man.

Most of the Commandments set forth in this chapter can help you trust your gut instincts—and stay safe—a little easier. Having a spare or two may just allow you to feel confident enough to leave this one in the dust. Not having sex on the first date keeps you from being alone with him. Skipping ex talk won't lead this guy to believe that you are vulnerable . . . Seeing a pattern here?

If your gut instinct tells you that there's something wrong, trust it and end this date. Be sure to call a friend and let her know what happened—and to make sure that you are not being followed once you leave. If you think you are, don't go directly home. Instead, head over to a populated area, call 911, and tell a cop your fears and where you are.

RelationTip: If he's creeping you out, take flight. Don't fight the feeling.

No. 9. Think Friendship First

If you go into every date situation thinking that you may make a new friend, you'll:

+ Take the pressure off yourself to "perform"

+ Be more likely to be like who you really are

+ Invest more time in the conversation than you will being worried if he likes you

+ Be less crushed if he doesn't call

The best relationships are based on friendship qualities: honesty, respect, having common morals and values. You already know you're attracted to him *that* way (heck, if you weren't, you wouldn't even *be* on this first date in the first place!). Now think about what you'd want in a friend and look for those qualities. And remember: Take your time to find them. Anything presented to you in those first few months may be Best Behavior buffed.

Bonus: If things don't work out, you end up with a new friend who may fix you up with someone who *will* work out.

No. 10. Have Fun

It's graduation night, and you just got your degree in Dateworthiness. You've got the knowledge. Now go forth and conquer with the confidence that if it doesn't turn into a second date, "it's not you . . . it's *him*!"

There you have it. The No-Fail Holy Grail, if you will, of essential rules—which lists "Have Fun" as your final task—which you should set in stone . . . or at least, set on your makeup table where you can see it just before leaving for that next first date.

RelationTip: Smiles. Laughter. Major turn-ons!

So . . . what happens when that first date becomes . . . the first few weeks . . . or even *months* of dating? If you're on your way out—we'll chat later about that.

However, if you are truly one of the Dateworthy diploma holders, thirsty for knowledge now, let's move on for some higher learning.

intelligent Part 4

open-minded responsible

funny self-aware

Great Date =
Possible Mate?

trusting sexy

magnetic self-respecting

confident

passionate

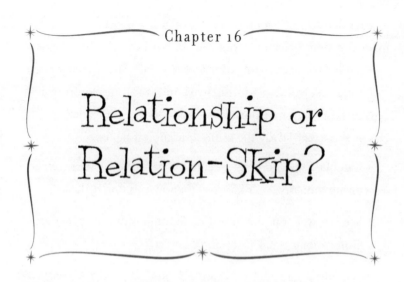

Chapter 16

Relationship or Relation-Skip?

So you've been first-dating up a storm. And you've dared to have spares . . . but . . . well . . . there is this *one* guy . . .

It's been quite a few dates already. Actually, it's been exactly three months since that very first great date . . . and yes, you *know* it's Best Behavior time and you know it's not love because supreme Dateworthy knowledge tells you that you can't hurry that but . . .

You're *crazy* about him.

And you can't help but start to wonder: Is he . . . *relationship-worthy?*

Actually, it's not such a bad thing to ponder at this time, if you agree with the following:

Fact 1: He's hung in there long enough for you to know he's not the "hit-it-and-run" playboy.

Fact 2: You've had enough time to really see scary signposts.

Fact 3: At three months, you are edging closer to crossing over from the Best Behavior Zone outskirts to the Reality Region.

Fact 4: He stands out in your Dare to Have Spares dating circle.

I'd say it's worth exploring why he's the one you're totally crushing on! My question to you is: Do you think he's totally crushing on *you*? I'd say the outlook is good if he has:

+ Exhibited the ability to execute the Non-Negotiables (respect, caring, honesty . . . I know you know this one by heart!).

+ Scored well on the five Cs: **C**ommunication, **C**hemistry, **C**ompatibility, and **C**onstant **C**ontact.

+ Started asking you, "What are you doing on . . ." for a date farther in the future that this coming Friday.

+ Introduced you to—and maybe had you come out with—the friends.

If you said "no" to any of the conditions above . . . I'm going to suggest you hold off on getting overly involved until he can meet them. However, if you scored a perfect "yes!". . . I'd say put your spares on hold for the next month and focus your attention on just this guy to see whether he's truly worth your attention, your time, and, possibly, your heart.

Let's examine the anatomy of the guy who is worthy of a relationship . . . or who is just a major relation-*skip*!

Relationship

He's worthy if:

+ He makes you feel good about yourself. That would seem obvious given that you're *crazy* about him but . . . not always the case

Dating Diary

I got "paired up" with Max for a friend's wedding (we were a part of a huge wedding party—he was a friend of the groom, I was a friend of the bride), and when I saw his picture, I couldn't wait for the rehearsal dinner. The attraction was instant and we started dating. After about two months, he kept hinting that he wanted to be exclusive, and I was hesitant . . . and told him perhaps down the road, but not now. He kept campaigning for the boyfriend slot, and I kept pushing him off, despite the fact that he really was pretty much my favorite guy in the group I was dating—the one I would blow off other dates for at the last minute. We fought about it and didn't speak for weeks.

One night I went out with a friend and ran into him and another girl. I was so upset, so broken up . . . and angry with myself for feeling that way because, after all, I had set the pace. I called him that night to see if we could actually get together and talk about an exclusive "trial." He said no.

"That should've been a decision you made because you really liked me, not because you had a jealous moment. That's a bad reason to be with someone." He was right. I never gave it a shot because I truly wasn't as into him as he was into me . . . and the knee-jerk reaction was because I couldn't stand the idea of losing his adoration.

this early in the game. Be sure that it's not what he does *with* you (the unbelievable places you go, the way he kisses) or what he does *for* you (with respect to feeling confident and self-worthfull to just be yourself) that's making you head over heels.

+ He's interested in your life. He doesn't just ask you about your day; he also remembers past conversations and follow-up questions ("Hey . . . whatever happened to that project you were so worried about getting in on time?"). Guys don't inquire just to be polite at this stage—they do because they really want to know.

+ His body language speaks louder than words. It's hard for a guy to admit he's into you this early in the game, especially if he's *really* into you, doesn't know how *you* feel, or doesn't want to get hurt. Instead, he finds ways to connect physically in a loving—but not necessarily sexual—way. If he's always grabbing for your hand when you're walking together, hugs you when he laughs, kisses your forehead, or touches your face . . . it's a sign he needs to be near you.

+ He doesn't seem to be dating others. Do you seem to go out a lot on Saturday nights (the traditional "couples' night") or have luck getting him to see you on a last-minute basis? Does he seem to get a little quiet when you tell *him* you have "plans" for the following night . . . or perhaps even seem to act too "casual" when he asks whom you're going out with ("Oh . . . are you seeing your friends? Meeting anyone there?")? Does he spend *quality* time with you? If he's spending so much time with you that you barely have time to date others . . . he doesn't either. The act of not seeing others without being asked says a lot about an underlying commitment without looking like he's rushing into commitment.

+ He opens up to you. Not necessarily about his feelings for you . . . but about things that are important to him, like if he's worried about his dad's health or frustrated with his inability to get ahead on his job. If he feels he can let down his "I'm da *man!*" mask even just a little, it means you've gained his trust.

+ He doesn't disappear during disagreements. There's no way two people can really start to have real intimacy without the discovery of something that they don't see eye to eye on. And one of the best indicators of whether you'd be a good couple is how you are able to compromise or agree to disagree. If he's all about working things out, it's because you mean enough for him to come-this-close to an apology (something men do only when absolutely necessary).

+ He's proud to have everyone know about you. He introduces you while holding your hand. If it's one of his friends, he or she will say, "I've heard so much about you!" As a matter of fact, it seems like everyone he knows who meets you knows you are the reason why he's been on cloud nine lately. He's almost wearing a sign that reads TAKEN for other girls (aka his spares) to see.

Just a note: If you have to really think about whether the above is true . . . it probably isn't, and you are projecting what you'd *like* him to be over what he really is.

RelationTip: If a guy tells you he's not capable of being in a relationship, or that you are too good for him, believe him and move on.

Relation-Skip

How's this for a no-brainer? He's a relation-skip if he doesn't meet the relationship criteria!

If only it were that easy.

Remember the fact that at this stage, you are *just* moving out of

Best Behavior Zone and into the realm of Reality Region. We're still early enough in the game that the guy you're nuts about is able to exhibit relationship-worthy qualities . . . while still not actually being relationship-worthy.

You know where that takes us? To a new set of scary signposts I call the three-month turnoffs.

The three-month turnoffs are behaviors that you need to keep an eye out for . . . that you might push away at this stage because you are completely, totally infatuated with him. (No kidding: Did you know that at the beginning of the courtship stage, there's a whole biology-chemistry kind of thing that the body actually goes through? That the head rush, the high, and the heart-pounding are caused by the endorphins rushing through your physical structure?)

The three-month turnoffs are the subtle cracks in his relationship-worthy mask that are just beginning to show as he works his Best Behavior tactics, and if you see one of them at this juncture, you need to turn off and take a back-to-dating detour.

That said, it's a relation-skip if, in between all the good stuff:

+ **He lies.** Even if you haven't actually caught him in a few . . . if you see him in action lying (on the phone, in person) and his lie is so good that, if you didn't know better, *you* would've believed him, you probably have already.

+ **He's financially irresponsible.** He's always broke and short on cash. There have been times that you've had to whip out your card on a date because his was "maxed out." Sure, he was appreciative . . . but I'm betting he's never paid you back. Guys who don't take responsibility or control over their money are guys who will be dependent on *you*.

Dating Diary

Hank was cute, funny, had a great job, and every date we went on was so much fun. We seemed to agree on everything and really enjoyed each other's company so much we hated for the date to end. I loved the way he seemed to really be into me. It was just such an amazing feeling to have someone I admired admire me!

So when he asked me not to see anyone else after three months, I didn't hesitate. When things started to get hot and heavy, I noticed he complained about his job a lot, and it turned out that it wasn't as great as he had made it out to be. And I noticed that he started nitpicking more about the way I dressed and about money issues. Funny, but in front of my friends, he'd be Mr. "A Round for Everyone on Me!" and in front of his friends, he'd complain about how having a girlfriend was a money pit.

Then . . . he hit me up for some money. A loan for $1,000 to be exact, because he had miscalculated his bills that month and needed to make car and rent payments. I told him I didn't feel comfortable, first of all because I couldn't afford to, and second, because my mom's Portuguese wisdom flashed into my head: "Men borrow from banks, not girlfriends." He got pissed and sullen. He broke up with me, but I felt like the "he" I had fallen for had left the building a long time ago.

+ **He's lazy.** Sure, he's crazy about you. But it seems that being kind and thoughtful and caring is all he has the energy for. When it comes to making goals and actually following through . . . well, he's always meaning to but just doesn't get to it. A man thinking about having a plan is not the kind of man you can trust to be a true partner in your hopes and dreams.

+ He's unreliable. You tell him to meet you at 7:00 . . . and you're asking "Where are you?" on your cell phone at 7:40. You ask him to remember to pick up the surprise birthday cake on the way to your place . . . and he not only forgets it, but he barely makes it in time to hide and yell "Surprise!" Stick with this guy and you might as well be single, because you are not going to be able to rely on him for anything.

And the worst one of all:

+ He cuts off important discussions with "whatever." He says it's because he doesn't want to fight. I say it's because he doesn't want to hear your opinion or to compromise.

+ RelationTip: The couple that <u>never</u> fights never expresses what they truly feel.

If you are happy to report that *he* seems like relationship material . . . let's take a little quiz and see if you two are couple-compatible!

Chapter 17

The Compatability Quiz

You're Dateworthy.

And so far . . . so is he.

However, your being Dateworthy and his being Dateworthy does not necessarily mean that you should be Dateworthy together! (That's kind of the equivalent of those friends who mean well, but only fix you up with someone on the basis of "She's single . . . he's single . . . perfect!")

> RelationTip: No matter how incredible you both are individually, it does not guarantee you will bring out the best in each other.

If you've decided to take the chance, get rid of your spares, and give a relationship with this seemingly good guy a try—

I'm rooting for you. But I also say . . . why leave it *all* to chance?

I'm about to suggest something that your guy is just going to hate. But the mere act of him going along with it suggests that he is certainly worth spending some valuable time and brain cells on.

I'm going to ask you two to take a compatibility quiz.

Here's how it works. He's hanging at your place, and you say, "I wanted to do this short couples quiz, but then I read that studies show that guys just aren't as good at doing them as girls—want to give it a shot anyway?"

I know, I know . . . we're appealing to that two-headed being ego again. But so what? It's not like that's a lie. . . .

Okay. Now grab two pens and two separate sheets of paper. Take turns doing the quiz, then compare results. Answer honestly and without too much analyzing—this is pretty simple! And let him know: There are no *right* answers . . . only honest ones.

The Quiz

1. When it comes to socializing, you prefer to:
   (a) Hang out with close friends and family.
   (b) Be around lots of new people.

2. When you have a problem, you often:
   (a) Keep it to yourself—you don't like to burden others.
   (b) Talk about it—you like getting feedback and ideas.

3. If someone had to describe your personality, they'd say you were:
   (a) The quiet, behind-the-scenes type.
   (b) The party spark plug.

4. Being alone:

    (a) Is good for the soul sometimes.

    (b) Is never fun.

5. It's more important to:

    (a) Enjoy what you do.

    (b) Make enough money to do the things you dream of doing.

6. If you have downtime, you would rather:

    (a) Curl up with a good book.

    (b) Invite a friend over to watch a movie.

7. When it comes to family:

    (a) You're very close and like to be involved with one another.

    (b) You love one another, but only get together for events.

8. You just got a big old bonus at work. You:

    (a) Spend a little, save a lot.

    (b) Spend a lot on something you really want, save the rest.

9. Your place is a mess. It:

    (a) Makes you crazy—you get to it ASAP.

    (b) Can wait—no one's coming over anytime soon.

10. The cashier just gave you too much change. You:

    (a) Tell her and give it back.

    (b) Give it back only if it's more than $5.

11. If you had to narrow it down to one word, you'd say you were:

    (a) An intellectual.

    (b) Creative.

12. Your friends:

    (a) Always like your dating choices.

    (b) Never get along with your dates.

Okay. Prepare to compare! Add up your answers and give yourselves one point for every one you answered the same.

Score   (you):   (him):

9–12: Extremely compatible! You two see eye to eye on a lot of important issues that crop up in relationships. Just make sure that your choices are based on your needs first, and not entirely on what you think the other person needs you to think.

5–8: Compatible, but needs compromise-ability. You have a lot in common, but there are times when you both need to do your own thing. If you two can find a way to take turns allowing the other to have a say—there's definitely a way to make this relationship work.

0–4: Opposites can attract—but if they don't find common ground, there may be grounds for a breakup. It's hard to let someone go when he or she is an incredible person, but best to do so that he or she—and you—can find their incredible compatible puzzle piece.

If you two scored terribly—the good news is that this is not a definite pass/fail on your relationship outlook. Actually . . . it may be just what you two need to analyze and discuss the things that you like to do, and see whether they are set in stone, or whether there's room for compromise.

✦

Compatibility is not about being the same person . . . it is, however, about sharing similar principles, goals, and values, and being able to appreciate each other's strengths and weak points. It's about opening yourself up to embracing someone's unique identity—without losing your own. It's what my mom has always called my dad:

"Similar . . . but different." And forty-five years later . . . it's certainly a Portuguese wisdom!

So . . . if you two find that as you continue on in your relationship, you don't have what it takes to be together?

You move on.

And you do that by being honest: "I don't really think that we have anything in common, and I think we need to break this off."

And firm: "I'm sorry, but I'm sure about this."

And kind: "It's not you . . . and it's not me . . . it's that 'us' *doesn't work.*"

And if you do seem to have what it takes to move forward? Perhaps we need to have a little talk about being exclusive!

Chapter 18

The Exclusive on Exclusivity

Thinking about kicking your dating relationship up a notch?

Wanting to change your status from "number one" to "only one"?

Don't tell me . . . tell him!

But before you do, you need to ask *yourself* the following questions:

+ Do we share the same relationship goals?

+ Are we both in a similar place in our lives?

+ Is this true commitment . . . or "convenient monogamy"?

+ Does the idea of bringing up exclusivity terrify me?

In case you're wondering . . . I'm looking for two "yesses," one "commitment, of course" and a "no" here. In that order. And in short order—I'll tell you why.

Relationship Goals

You would like to get married while you're still young enough to birth a baby or two. He'd like to get married someday, but not anytime soon, and *especially* not until he's had a chance to do that cross-country-tour-on-a-Harley thing he and his friends have been talking about since high school graduation a decade ago.

Call me crazy, but, I'm thinking—these are relationship goals that aren't exactly meshing seamlessly.

If you and your sweetie haven't yet discussed relationship goals, you absolutely must do it before you even consider making your relationship an exclusive one. Exclusivity has to do with compatibility. If you two don't share the same relationship goals and vision for your future, then it's a major mistake to get your heart tangled up with this person.

RelationTip: If you're not headed for the same goal, then you should remain on opposite teams.

And ladies . . . if he says he does *not* want the same things you do . . . *believe* him. Do not even start thinking, "Oh, well, he says that he doesn't want marriage now, but once we've been together a little longer and he falls deeper in love with me, he'll see the error of his ways." If I had a dime for every letter I got from women who wasted years waiting for him to alter his not-headed-to-the-altar thinking . . . and a nickel for every note from a newly dumped female who "accidentally" got pregnant mid-marriage despite the no-babies deal . . . well, I'd have a whole lot of dimes and nickels.

But if you do share a vision, now you need to figure out if it's on the same time line.

Relationship Timing

You both want to be married and have kids. But you're still in grad school and want to wait till you get your degree; your boyfriend, older and established, doesn't want to wait any longer to start having a family.

Goals: compatible. Timing: incompatible.

Just as it is important to ask, "*What* are your relationship goals?" it's also imperative to ask, "And *when* are you planning to start executing them?"

✦ RelationTip: When you meet the right person at the wrong time, you may be tempted to make the wrong choice for what you think is the right reason: love.

Becoming exclusive when you both know that you have different life needs and timing is only delaying—and worsening—the eventual breakup you will have when you realize that love does *not* conquer all issues.

Commitment . . . or Convenience?

You've been dating this guy a while, and he's pretty great. Unlike the other guys you have gone out with, he's the only one who wants to be exclusive. You figure . . . hey, isn't that what dating is all about? To keep doing it until you find someone who wants you? You go for it.

Girl, if I've just described how you're feeling, you should not only *not* be exclusive—you need to flip back a few chapters and re-connect with the Dateworthiness you so obviously have lost.

The point of dating is to keep meeting new guys, and opening yourself up to finding a guy whom you truly and deeply care to be with. You know what I mean—Mr. Right versus Mr. Right for the Moment.

RelationTip: Never settle just so that you can settle down.

Remember: True romance comes only out of true commitment. Believe in your Dateworthiness enough to know that this guy isn't going to be the only guy who ever falls for you. Why should *he* be the only one to experience the giddiness that comes with falling for someone?

Too Terrified

This is not the army, chickie—the don't ask, don't tell policy definitely does not work when it comes to relationships!

Ask yourself why you're terrified—is it because you don't trust your judgment? If so, I say *nonsense*. If you've come this far, and you've done the homework, you are a fabulous new Date-worthy person who should follow up on her gut instinct about this great guy.

Is it because you don't think he's on the same page? If that's because after all this time, he's still seeing other girls . . . and has never called you his girlfriend . . . I'd say, girlfriend, you're probably right. Skip the exclusive and go right for the personal ads.

Dating Diary

I was completely nuts over Anthony, a lawyer who had dreams of one day becoming a judge, packaged in tall, dark, Italian stud-muffin, sexy looks. He lived and practiced in upstate New York, but came into Manhattan all the time to take in plays, do the nightlife, and enjoy the restaurants, and I was more than happy to be right there with him. We kind of naturally fell into an exclusive situation where we both let each other know we just weren't interested in seeing anyone else.

One day, over some especially delicious bow-tie pasta, I commented, "Life just doesn't get any better than this!"

And he said, "Sure it does . . . eventually you grow up, get married, move to the country, pop out a few kids, and live happily ever after."

I laughed. "Yeah, right. Maybe for someone else, but not me!"

He seemed shocked. "Really? You actually want to stay here for the rest of your life?"

"Well . . . that's the vision. Me in Manhattan and no kids," I replied.

Once you know what's making you terrified, I say start writing down the reasons why and take a good look. If they are reasons that make perfect non-exclusivity sense, reexamine the relationship and see whether what's needed is more casual dating time . . . or just to keep it casual and keep dating.

+

So that's the exclusive on exclusivity. If it sounds right for you, I say—get right to it! Only time will tell whether you two will even-

As we discussed the issue more and more, I realized that if I wanted to keep this one, I was going to have to accept his vision of what my future looked like. I felt sick to my stomach and asked him to take me home. There was major tension in the car. We said good night . . . and I went upstairs.

Several hours later, my doorbell was ringing frantically. It was Anthony and I let him up. He reached into his pocket and took out a black velvet box and opened it to the biggest pear-shaped diamond I had ever seen.

He said, "If you change your mind now, and tell me that you can picture yourself in my dream, it's yours."

I took the box. Tried on the ring. And then I gave it back.

"Anthony, we're not just not sharing similar dreams. I love you but I don't want to marry you now . . . and I don't think I can promise you a future with kids and the country either."

Needless to say, that was a really painful breakup.

---

tually pick up a copy of my second book, *Ringworthy*. . . . (And when I say time, I *do mean* time—as in you both need to share at least once: every holiday in a year, a birthday, a family function, *and* a vacation away).

RelationTip: Love come easy is love that goes away easy.

Do you remember when we started this journey together, waaaaay back in the beginning when you picked up this book, intrigued about the cover's concept of being "Dateworthy" and getting the relationship you want?

I've got a secret: You are now not only ready to get the relationship you want . . . you've also gotten a bonus: a relationship you needed—the brand-new confident one with yourself!

In order to become Dateworthy, you had to find your own self-worthfullness, the confidence to know that you are the best you can be. When you feel great about yourself ("I like me, I *really like me!*"), you are more apt to hold out and take your time to find someone who deserves your love . . . and gives you the love that you deserve.

So, congratulations, and big hugs to you. Now, will you get out there and apply all that education already? Geez. I didn't support your Dateworthy education to have you just sitting around. Get out and get *dating*!

intelligent Part 5

open-minded responsible

funny self-aware

Readers' Most Frequently Asked Questions

trusting sexy

magnetic

self-respecting

confident

passionate

Chapter 19

Reader Q&A

I think the reason why my column in *USA WEEKEND* is so popular is because the reader dilemmas that I resolve are chosen based on how often that issue pops up in my inbox and mailbag. The audience wants to see matters that they relate to resolved. And not only are they happy to get a straight answer . . . they feel a little bit better knowing that they are not the only ones who have had to deal with that kind of problem in their lives.

In that spirit, I waded through thousands of letters, and tried to narrow down the top dating questions that I see over and over again . . . and shared them with you

You'll notice that amongst the many letters from fabulous females from across the country are a few from . . . two-headed beings! (See? I *told* you that they are able to ask for direction!) Like I said earlier, guys *do* want to have relationships, and I think these Q&As will give you a little insight into what's going on when the heart blocks the route from Gray Matter HQ to Reaction Central!

So, kick back, relax, and take a look at the top dating dilemmas . . . and if you see yourself in one of 'em, I hope the advice helps you through it!

Dating and Sex

Fairfax, VA: I'm having trouble finding a guy who is willing to wait longer than the first date to have sex. I don't meet guys in bars—mostly at the gym and other places. I am not a prude, but I am not one of those "girls gone wild" either. What's the deal?

DH: Girlfriend, do what I did. I said, "You know, I don't hit the sheets on the first date." Sounding lighthearted—but firm—will make a guy who *wants* a girl stick around.

Newport News, VA: I made a cardinal mistake and went a bit too far physically with someone whom I had just met. I really like him and will be going on a second date with him this week, but I'm not sure how to approach the physical side of the relationship.

DH: When you go out again, say, "I had the best time on Friday—you really swept me off my feet. Would you mind if this time, we do a lot of talking and take things back a step for a bit?" If he asks why, say, "Because I think you are worth getting to know as a person, and I want us to crave each other so badly, next time things will be even hotter." Good luck!

New York, NY: I have just started dating someone and would like to begin a sexual relationship. Is it too much to ask to have a man have a full checkup before sex? I have been out of the dating game for a while, and this subject just seems both overwhelming and embarrassing.

DH: Let's just put it this way: If you're too embarrassed to talk about STDs, you're not ready to handle having a sexual relationship! STDs are health- and life-threatening. If you two have been getting closer and closer to a physical relationship, the best way to break the ice is to give him a present—like some fun-wrapped condoms from condomania.com—and get the dialogue going.

Orlando, FL: Does playing hard to get ever really work in the long run, or is it short-lived?

DH: It depends on the definition of "hard to get." If it means, "I won't sleep with just anyone and be discriminate," then I'm with you. Being choosy about who you give yourself to is a smart choice in the dating game; abstaining from immediate pleasure is something most women don't do and I believe should do. We ladies need to get back to expecting *courtship*.

New York, NY: How long should you wait in a new relationship to have sex?

DH: Wait until you've been dating long enough that you know personal hygiene and you feel comfortable enough to ask, "So . . . what's up with that sore down there?" And, of course, *never* on a first date!

Moving the Relationship Forward

Seattle, WA: How do you deal with a shy guy? I have been hanging out with one who hints that he likes me but won't take the next step. I see him three times a week at various gatherings, and we usually hang out afterward, but the relationship is progressing very slowly. I'm not confident enough to make the next move and feel that it is up to him.

DH: Listen, you may not be confident, but it sounds like this guy is a whole lot *less* confident than you are! That said, if you really want to start something with him, it's up to you to make that first move: *Ask him out!*

Washington, DC: I have often asked women out whom I have met during the course of daily life, such as the gym, the bus, etc. When they say no, the situation often gets awkward as I still see them pretty much every day. Is it a bad idea to ask women out in this kind of setup?

DH: A terrific question! Actually, it's totally acceptable—and smart—to approach a woman you're attracted to in everyday places. The key? Keep the approach casual. Try, "You know, I see you all the time on the bus/at the gym, and I was wondering, would you like to have coffee sometime?" If she says no, just smile and say in a very light, good-natured way, "Okay—just thought I'd give it a shot!" It's not an awkward situation unless you think too much into it—shrug it off, nod in passing, and turn your thoughts elsewhere.

Los Angeles, CA: I've been going out with this guy for a few months, and it has been better than any of my other relationships.

How do you know if you are really in love with someone or whether it's puppy love, a crush, or lust? I want to tell him how I feel . . . just don't know what to call it.

DH: Lust is an immediate feeling of attraction, an "omigod-I-must-get-in-his-pants" kind of thing. A crush is where you think you like someone based on little contact, and it's usually one-sided. *Love* . . . aaaah! . . . is based on getting to know each other, and being treated with honesty, caring, respect, and kindness. If he makes you happy, and you're pretty sure he's feeling the same way about you, don't plan on saying "I love you," but do allow it to pop out in a wonderful moment.

Cleveland, OH: I have been dating a guy for a little over a year. What are some good indicators of whether we are meant to be?

DH: Here's a short list of things to consider:

Have you spent lots of time together? The more you do, the more you'll learn how your intended reacts in difficult life situations. Also, you need to get to know each other's close friends; they are a huge indicator of what someone is really into.

Do you know each other's goals, values, beliefs? If not, now's the time to discuss a list of no-compromise situations. In addition to big issues like sex, religion, kids, and money, don't forget hot-button topics like household chores.

Are the people close to you happy about your relationship? If they can best describe it as loving, honest, respectful, and supportive, you're on the right track.

San Diego, CA: I like this "special someone" and would like to meet him again. I proposed going out for dinner once, but he said he was busy. It has been a while since I asked him. Should I take this "busy" as "not interested" or really busy? How can I give this another try without being pushy?

DH: Ask him out again. Say, "Hey—just wondering—do you have any free time this week to grab a bite or coffee or a movie?" If he says no, then ask, "Oh, okay . . . think you'll have some free time next week?" If he comes up with a negative excuse, let it go. A guy who is interested *will* be able to find time in a two-week time span, no matter *how busy* he is.

Dating Etiquette

Cincinnati, OH: What is an appropriate Christmas gift for a man you have been dating casually for a few months?

DH: Think about some of the things he is passionate about—a particular sports team, for example—and see if you can get tickets for him. Or, if he's into music, pick up a CD and pair it with a bottle of wine and a note saying, "Let's share. . . ." Does he ever complain about how long it's been since he's had a home-cooked meal? Make him one! The point: Think about the things he's shared with you, and come up with something that indulges his interests. He'll appreciate knowing that you truly listen to him!

San Francisco, CA: What do you think about dating a guy that has a rather "colorful" past? He's been in trouble with the law, done some jail time, sold drugs, worked as a male escort, etc, etc. You name it, he's done it. Of course, that was fifteen years ago, and when you talk to him about it today, he shakes his head in disbelief at how irresponsible he was in his youth (he's thirty-nine now). Today, he's such a thoughtful, caring, responsible guy, you'd never guess his past if he didn't tell you. But I'm having a hard time getting past it. What should I do?

DH: Would I date this guy? No, but that's purely a personal thing. I do think it's a good sign that your guy was so honest about a past he's ashamed of. The most important thing here is to be quite sure that he truly is embarrassed and reformed, and to find out what he did to work on himself to make sure he'd never fall into this crazy life again. You should also be very adamant about his having an AIDS test. If he's truly reformed, and cares about you, you won't see resistance to your questions and request.

Atlanta, GA: I am new to dating and would like to know who should pay for the first few dates. Is it shared, or is the man expected to pay?

DH: On casual lunches with non-dates, you should always offer to ante up half, but on first dates, I personally like men to pay unless I'm the one who did the asking out and pursuing.

Union, NJ: Is it better to ask for an e-mail address or a phone number when meeting someone you're interested in?

DH: It's always best to just say, "I'd love to see you again. How can I get in touch with you?" The reason: You'll know where you stand. The person who gives you digits wants to talk to you again; the person giving you an e-mail isn't so sure!

Oakland, CA: How can I politely tell a guy that I am not ready to give him my telephone number/e-mail address yet?

DH: If you like the guy, say, "I don't give my phone number on the first date, but I'll take yours!" If it's a guy you don't like, be honest, but be kind: "You know what? I think you're sweet, but I don't want to pursue a relationship right now."

Baltimore, MD: I am thirty-three years old, and the guy I've been dating for three months is twenty-six. Any advice for May-December romances?

DH: There's nothing wrong with an age difference as long as both of you are adults and out of school. I say, as long as you are both honest and fair and loving and respectful and crazy for each other, *have a great time.* Your only consideration: the biological clock. Don't rush into anything just because you may want a baby.

Phoenix, AZ: After how many dates or how much time should the labels boyfriend/girlfriend be used?

DH: The number is totally different with every couple. The way you know is that, over time, one of you is going to bring up the topic to the other of being monogamous. If it's a yes, then it's official you are boy/girlfriends.

Boise, ID: After a date when the woman asks me to call her, how long should I wait? I want to sound interested without sounding desperate.

DH: Don't wait days to call her, or you will look like the typical guy trying to make her sweat. Call the next day, and be prepared with a few ideas about what you'd like to do on your next date so that the conversation will flow. And be sure to start the conversation with, "I had a great time the other night, and hoped we could go out again!"

Bridgeport, CT: My boyfriend of three months mentioned to me that his ex, who he says is a horrible person, was the best sex he ever had. Why would he say something so hurtful when we are in the middle of an argument?

DH: Get rid of him. The first few months of a relationship are supposed to be the *romance* period, when people are on their best behavior, trying to impress each other. That he can say something so insensitive and emotionally abusive this early on in the relationship is a *major red flag*—even if it was in anger. (Especially so—people who get angry and look to hurt on a personal level don't get better without help.) End this, chalk it up to a learning experience, and find a man who would never dream of hurting you this way. Big hugs to you—I hate that you had to feel that pain.

Moving Too Fast

Houston, TX: I'm desperately trying to get the timing right in my relationship. We've been going out for about three months, and all is well. We both admitted to each other that we tend to fall fast in relationships. Moving in has been discussed, and a gap of at least six months of dating has been agreed on. Do you think that is enough time? I know we have to talk about all of the money, kids, chores stuff. I just don't want to be too quick and base things on any other reason than it being right.

DH: Whoa, slow down! It's been three months. I truly believe everyone is on their *best* behavior the first three to five months in a relationship, and then . . . all the weird little stuff starts to come out. You're both smart cookies, realizing that you have a tendency to "fall fast." With that in mind, stay put in your own places, and see where the relationship is in another six months. If you still feel there's a true connection, *then* start exploring deeper commitment issues. Talking, that is, from separate apartments. Good luck.

Nashville, TN: If a man seems interested in you and then you become very close very fast only to have him give you the "I like you, but . . ." speech, is it possible that he is afraid, or is it actually that he was never interested to begin with?

DH: Most likely he *was* interested, and as he got to know you, was no longer interested "that" way. Don't take offense or take it to heart: Just because you're not his dream girl doesn't mean you're not the fantasy of at least a hundred other guys!

Sheboygan, WI: I met a girl a month ago, and we spend almost all of our spare time together. Do you think it's too early for us to "officially" be in love? When does one know that it is truly love and not the excitement and lust of something new?

DH: Definitely too early. A good rule of thumb: The first three or four months of a relationship is the total honeymoon, Best Behavior Zone. Usually, after four months, a more real picture of who you are with will start to emerge. If you're still together for a year, and you still love being together, then I'd vote that it's possible for you to be "officially" in love! Don't worry about that label, though. Just enjoy the ride and the excitement and see if time takes you there!

Yuma, AZ: I'm just starting to date again after a messy breakup about a year ago. I really like the person I'm seeing now, but I really don't know how to act around him. Is it because I am not ready?

DH: A breakup can certainly shake your confidence and bring your paranoia of the opposite sex up about twelve points! Most likely you're uneasy because you're worried about being set up for another hurt. I'm also betting that you really like him, and being able to feel that again is scary. Here's what you do: Take things slow, relax, and be honest. When you go out and you feel that things are a little weird or quiet, laugh and say, "I thought they said that dating was like riding a bicycle—that you never forget. I'm totally lousy at this!" Open the door to discussing the fact that you've just started dating again after a huge breakup—don't, however, talk about your ex. Instead, ask your date if he's ever gone through this, and make a joke about another bad breakup you had in the seventh grade that had you just as nervous. Trust me: This guy will be relieved to know your anxiousness is due to that and not to his personality!

At-Work Romance

Santa Monica, CA: Is getting involved with people you work with a good idea? I'm thinking about it but am not sure what to do. *Please help!*

DH: We Americans spend the biggest part of our day at a job. It's hard *not* to get involved! That said, here are a few things to consider:

+ Does your office have a no-dating policy? If so, hold back: Losing a job in this harsh economy is not a good thing.

+ Do you work right next to each other, or do either one of you report to each other? The last thing you need is a bad breakup with someone you have to see daily. If this is the scenario, don't make the move. If these two considerations are not worries, then it's time to think again: Do you know him well enough to know he isn't a psycho, or hasn't been in past office relationships? Is he *really* worth sacrificing a job for? If you say yes to these two questions, go for it, but proceed slowly and keep things light for a while.

Tampa, FL: I'm trying to get the guy I like at work to notice me. I asked him out to lunch, but I still don't think he got the hint! Is there anything else I can do to make him see I want him to ask me out?

DH: How about just coming out and saying, "Hey—want to do a movie and dinner sometime next week?" There's nothing wrong with being blunt . . . as long as you have truly thought out your work situation and what a failed relationship would mean to your job. If he says no? Chalk it up to that weird chemistry thing, don't take it personally, and move on. I'm betting you'll have a good response, though: He did, after all, accept your invite to lunch!

Chicago, IL: I am attracted to a girl who works in my office building. I have no reason to talk to her, so what do I say when I approach her?

DH: Start by smiling at her and saying hello. If she's receptive to that, walk over and ask her if you can buy her coffee tomorrow morning. If she likes you, she'll say yes, or suggest lunch. If not, she'll shoot you down, and then you should treat yourself to something nice for being so brave.

Dating Behavior Patterns

Atlanta, GA: Why do I keep meeting men who are cheap and want someone to take care of them?

DH: When you keep meeting the same type of man over and over, it's time to stop and realize: "Hey, I'm the common denominator here. What signals am I sending out? Is there a type of guy I keep being attracted to?"

If so, let yourself talk to or be approached by a totally different type of guy. Stage your own personality intervention—get trusted friends to tell you what *they* see you doing over and over in the man department. You may learn a lot about yourself, and it will help you open your eyes and end your loser run!

Austin, TX: I never seem to have a problem going out on a first date, having a great time, and making a new friend, but it never seems to work out in trying to get to the next date. Why is it that the nice guys always finish last? Every time I try to be nice, like sending someone soup when they are sick or anything like that, I never get a thank-you.

DH: First . . . you need to sit down with a trusted female friend, relay your first-date conversation and behaviors, and figure out what's turning girls off! And, as for the nice-guy thing . . . yes, nice guys finish last when they keep going after the type of girls who truly want to deal with a bad boy and all the bad behavior that goes with it. There are a lot of girls out there who would appreciate a nice guy—keep trying!

Las Vegas, NV: I meet lots of women who are interested in me but whom I feel no physical attraction for. On the other hand, those women I do feel attracted to are not interested in me. This is very frustrating, and I feel trapped in a sort of "no man's land." Am I setting my standards too high? Shouldn't love include physical attraction? And all these women whom I would like to date yet write me off, have I not met their standards? Please let me know what you think.

DH: Let's take your questions one by one.

1. You *may* be setting your standards way too high—or perhaps way off base from who you *truly are*. If you're looking for the supermodel type who's only looking for a jet-setting money guy and you've got beer pockets but think a good heart will get you over, it's time to rethink that plan. Take a good look in the mirror, make a list of who you think you are, and have your friends look at the list and either add to it . . . or alter your perceptions a bit!

2. Yes, love includes physical attraction, but physical attraction could mean a lot of things: One guy is attracted to great legs, another guy may be a great face and skin junkie, and yet another may love a big beautiful woman. However, if you want to open up your possibilities, it may be best to come up with more than *one* characteristic that turns you on.

One more thing: The fact that you even asked means you have an open mind and are willing to learn—very attractive traits in a guy. Keep on looking, keep yourself open, and I guarantee you'll find someone!

Dating and Friends

Los Angeles, CA: I'm in love with a good friend of mine and don't know what's wrong with him. We went on a date once, and things were going well. We talked a few times on the phone, but then all of a sudden it just stopped. I still see him around, but things aren't the same. Is it because he doesn't feel the same way I do, or is he just shy?

DH: I'm betting he realized there was no chemistry, and he's avoiding you until this dating phase passes, and then will ease back into being "just friends." You can help facilitate this if you stop wondering what happened and why, and just call him and say, "Listen, things are weird between us. I don't want to lose our friendship. If you're trying to find a way to end the romantic thing without hurting me, the best way is to tell me, so we can discuss it and resolve never to bring it up again!"

Philadelphia, PA: I'm female and have lots of male friends in my circle, so I meet lots of guys. I'm not interested in dating anyone, only in new friends. This always gets misread into, "I'll have a chance later," which makes for a lot of discomfort and misunderstandings. I'm nice and friendly, but this gets misinterpreted, too. I must be giving the wrong signals, but I don't know what they are. Any advice for someone who is happy with the single life and not interested in dating?

DH: Know that saying, "Friends make the best lovers?" Well, what's happening here is that, even though you make things clear from the get-go (you are, right?), as your guy friends get to know and love you, their heart pushes them to give romance a shot. Just be kind, remind them that you are still in single, no-dating mode, and if any of them can't deal with just the friendship, be prepared to back off on hanging out for a while. Incidentally, I'm curious—single and *not* dating? Why not? Dating everyone and anyone is half the fun of *being* single!

Nashua, NH: My friends don't like the guy I'm dating. Do you have any advice?

DH: Do you know *why* everyone hates him? Very often, your friends—that is, if they are good friends with your best interests at heart—can see things you can't because your heart is in the way. Listen up, be honest about their reasons, and reevaluate your relationship if what they say makes sense.

Omaha, NE: I broke up with my girlfriend a little over a year ago. We both agreed to be friends and, I thought, we had been successful in doing so. Since then I have dated other people, though she has not seemed to have much luck in her dating efforts. About three months ago I started to become very close to someone, and this new relationship shows great promise. My problem is that within the last month or so my old girlfriend has become very aggressive in letting me know that she would like for us to try again. She knows I am in another relationship, which might be why she is starting to apply pressure. I care a great deal for her as a friend, but I am beginning to believe the best thing I can do for her is tell her I do not want to see her anymore. I am thinking that this might help her get over our previous relationship and move on to something better for her. Do you think this is the right way to go? Why is it so hard to be friends with someone in this type of situation?

DH: Being honest is less cruel than saying nothing and letting her think you're coming around. I'm a huge believer in avoiding friendship after a breakup, particularly because there's usually one in that relationship who didn't really want the breakup in the first place, and that person would use the "friendship" as a hopeful re-launch back to the way things used to be. Tell her it's truly over, that you have met someone else, and apologize for hurting her. Be firm, but be kind.

Tampa, FL: Lately things with a very good friend have been taking a turn toward something more than friends. Neither one of us is brave enough to discuss it, although we both hint at it. We are both so scared of getting hurt, but I'm interested and I'm pretty sure that he is, too. What do we do?

DH: It's scary when you want to take your friendship to a romantic level but you're afraid to ruin the friendship you already have. However, here's what's scarier: No one makes a move, and one of you meets someone new, and the one left behind always wonders, "What if?" I say, ask him out!

Dayton, OH: I recently told my best friend that I wanted to be more than friends. She handled it better than I thought she would until she gave me the "You're a nice guy, but . . ." line. I've heard this line so many times that to me it means that I'm nice enough to have as a friend, but not nice enough to date. Is there something wrong with me that I keep hearing this? Is there something that I can do about it?

DH: I'm betting that what's wrong isn't who you are—it's who you're going for! Think about the girls who have told you

you're too nice: Are they party girls who are not looking to settle down, looking for bad boys and a type that you don't fit? Perhaps what you need to do is try to say hello to a girl whom you wouldn't normally go after—someone just as pretty, but in a more conservative, together way—and try your luck from there. I'm betting you're a terrific guy—the kind that girls wished they *had* fallen for after getting burned several times. A great way to change up whom you date is to go to an online dating site and submit a profile that states you are looking for a girl who wants a nice guy—I bet you'll be flooded with replies. Good luck!

Dayton, OH: Is there a good way to tell your best friend that you would like to become more than just friends? We've been friends for years and now she lives three hours away. I could care less about the distance. But I don't know how to bring it up without making things awkward between us. I'm afraid she's not going to react to it well.

DH: If you're afraid she's not going to react well, most likely that means you shouldn't make a move. Being someone's best friend means you really know what they're about, and how they feel. If your gut tells you that this confession could wreck the friendship you already have, then you need to really think this through and decide if that relationship is worth losing. If you absolutely, positively cannot stand it another moment, tell her, but be prepared that it might not end well.

Dallas, TX: I've had a few dates recently with a guy who once dated a friend of mine. It's been over with them for about six months, but I still feel a little guilty. I would talk to him about this, but don't what to come across as paranoid.

DH: This is an issue that you should first discuss with your friend. My question: Is your guilt stemming from the fact that you haven't exactly been forthcoming with your buddy about those few dates? Bet it is . . .

Dating and the Internet

Los Angeles, CA: I just started getting to know a guy I met on an Internet dating site, and we have a lot in common. Overall, he seems like a great guy (we're both in our forties), as we're still in the preliminary stages of getting to know each other by phone. The only problem is that when we talk, and our talk is lively, he never seems to ask me very many questions about myself—rather, he mostly talks about himself. Do you think that this may be out of nervousness, or is it a sign of something else I should be aware of?

DH: Give the phone conversations a little more time—it really could be nerves, and seeing that the telephone is truly an instrument that women are more comfortable with than men (let's face it—a phone is a *communication* tool!), he may be trying to fill up dead space. He may also be worried that if he asks too *you* too many questions, you may feel unsafe. Next conversation, say in a light tone, "I know so much about you now, except for what you would like to know about me! I don't mind if you ask me a few questions. . . ." If that doesn't change things, sign off from this guy.

San Francisco, CA: What are the telltale signs of players on Internet dating sites?

DH: A true player will push you to get involved, hit it, and get out fast. Anyone who is rushing you to see him/her, or is already proclaiming love and devotion just because of your letters, beware!

San Francisco, CA: I know that you are a proponent of Internet dating, but what do you think of someone who e-mails you only once a week after you've established contact? Is this person a player, or taking their time, or looking for something better in the meantime?

DH: I am huge fan of Internet dating, in conjunction with meeting people on your own and through fix-ups. The once-a-week e-mailer is someone who is dating more than one person—early on, that's acceptable. However, if this person professes love and other serious stuff, and sticks to that schedule, be wary and question it. Trust me, just as in "real life" dating, someone who only needs to speak to you on a once-a-week schedule is someone who's not entirely into you . . . yet.

New York, NY: I met a guy online and have purchased a ticket to fly out to meet him. He seems quite normal and sweet, unlike the last guy I got involved with (whom I also flew out to meet, which turned out to be a disaster). I ran a background check on him and it came out clean. I'm supposed to fly out on Friday, and I haven't heard from him in a few days—no call, no e-mail, nothing. He's got a job that requires him to arrive at work very early for the stock market opening, and he's told me that if he doesn't communicate, it's because he's a trader who spends his day on the phone, so if he's busy he can't talk. Fair enough. But should I worry that I haven't heard from him? Am I overreacting? If I haven't heard from him by Thursday, should I cancel the trip?

DH: Background checks only clear a potential date of any reported criminal activity—it does not, however, vouch for character.

Relationship Q & A

I have many friends who have met online and married; unfortunately, they were all supposedly "happily married" at the time when they were cruising the online personals! My question is what are the statistics for online dating being the cause of breaking up families? —S. M., Tennessee

While there aren't a lot of long-term, concrete stats available on Internet infidelity, you don't really need scientific research to know that the husband or wife who is cruising for dates in Cyberspace—or anyplace—is not happily married to begin with. While it's true that more and more couples are seeking counseling or breaking up due to cheating that began online, the true reason for the infidelity has less to do with technology than old-fashioned human emotions: Someone in the relationship was unfulfilled and looked elsewhere.

The bottom line? Even though the Internet makes it easier to reach out and touch someone, it's up to the person at the keyboard whether or not to actually make the connection.

That said, I think you need to cancel this airline ticket. First face-to-face meetings should *never* take you far away from your home and should *not* entail an expensive airline ticket, with effort only on one person's end. The fact that he's incommunicado with you before a flight says to me that this guy's not only *not* interested . . . he's probably a little freaked out by what seems to be your desperation to meet. Cancel this trip, take the financial hit, and consider ending this relationship.

St. Louis, MO: Am I crazy to forgo a local relationship to pursue a "seemingly" more meaningful online relationship?

DH: If you're already looking around online and elsewhere, that means the local relationship wasn't for you in the first place! Do go ahead and check out your online potential relationship, but do the right thing and break up locally first.

Kansas City, KS: I have a question about Internet dating. I've always heard that guys love the chase. Does that mean if you contact a man online that it already makes you the "aggressor"?

DH: No, actually, with online dating, contacting is only half the game. Eventually, *someone* has to say, "Let's meet," and studies show that 85 percent of guys online are usually the ones to make that move, so . . . if you're truly paranoid about making a move, contact him, and wait to see if he does the actual asking! Incidentally, contact and asking out is not the kind of "aggressive" guys who like a "chase" are referring to.

Indianapolis, IN: I recently have been attending some speed-dating events. I match with quite a few women, but when I get their e-mail addresses and write to them, I get no response. Any suggestions on what to put in the e-mails? I have been just staying generic and using the "Hi. Hope you had fun. Hope to hear back from you" kind of thing.

DH: Speed dating—whether it's eight-minute or three-minute—is basically a physical connection, and is not as effective as doing the Internet dating thing, where you connect emotionally and mentally *first*. If you'd still like to pursue the speed-dating challenge, it's important that you jot down some notes about the girl before contacting her ("likes bowling, vegetarian") so that your e-mails can be more personalized ("Hey, I was thinking that perhaps we could do a little lighted-pin bowling, then follow it up at this vegetarian restaurant a friend recommended"). Personalization—as well as an actual, suggested date that touches on her interests—may help your e-mails. Good luck!

Long-Distance Dating

Centreville, VA: I've recently started conversing with a very nice person from Ohio. We seem to like each other from our phone conversations (daily), and we like the photos we've seen of each other. Any recommendations on long-distance relationships?

DH: Take it slowly and cautiously. Meet the first one or two times at a halfway point (bring a friend with you for safety reasons, and encourage him to do the same). Then visit each other (stay at a hotel, don't plan on staying at each other's homes) a few times, take a vacation together, see how it feels to spend time. Save relocation talk for some time way in the future when you both are seriously committed.

Washington, DC: What does it take to make long-distance relationships work, and how do you know when to throw in the towel?

DH: Long-distance love is difficult and dependent on three things: communication, trust, and, most important, the ability to be honest about your own feelings. The communication part is where you go over the details about what each of you wants and needs to keep this love alive. Now is the time to let each other know just how seriously you're taking this relationship. Some key questions to ask: Are we seeing each other exclusively, or can we date others? How will we keep in touch? Do we have enough money to finance visits? What is the ultimate goal of this relationship? How long are we giving the long-distance thing before one of us has to relocate? And which one would it be?

Then the trust issue: Will your boyfriend honor the promises you've made to each other? If your relationship is new (less than a year old), or if your partner has given you cause in the past to suspect cheating, then the distance will not be kind to your peace of mind.

And be brutally honest with yourself: To make a go of it, there has to be serious commitment on both sides. Are you in love, just "in like," or merely maintaining the relationship as a security blanket? Will not having regular physical contact become an issue? Once you've gone through the consideration process, if you're still game to take a stab at long-distance love, go for it. Finding—and keeping—true love is worth the work.

Princeton, NJ: I met a girl on vacation who lives across the country. We had a really great time together for a couple of days. She is the coolest girl I have met in years, but I am not sure how to approach the whole long-distance thing. On top of that, she said she just got out of a long-term relationship. Any suggestions?

DH: Don't expect too much: Summer long-distance love is one of those very fleeting things. Your best bet: Ask if you two can be friends, and e-mail each other, and get to know each other on that level. If it's meant to be more, you'll know in the future. In the meantime, continue to date on your turf.

Dating with Kids

Louisville, KY: I've been dating a wonderful man for a short time—five weeks—and he has three children, ages fourteen, eleven, and eight. I don't have children yet. What do you think is an appropriate period of time to date before introducing children to a new significant other? I don't want to rush things at all, just looking for some advice!

DH: If you and he are seeing each other on a regular basis, there's nothing wrong with him introducing his new "friend." Go on an outing with them, keeping physical/intimate contact *out* of the time you're together. Five weeks is a little soon; give this another few months, and then do start becoming a buddy they see on an occasional basis. Just a little word o' warning: His having kids means you're going to have to deal with some canceled-last-minute dates and possibly some odd power trips. If he's worthy, it's a learning experience, so just know in advance and be prepared for the ride.

Allentown, PA: I'm dating a divorcing man, and his teens have not dealt well with the divorce. Any tips for the first time I meet them?

DH: Be prepared to be tested, and be prepared not to be liked! However, if you approach the situation with an attitude of

Relationship Q & A

I'm a recently divorced dad with custody of two girls, ages six and nine. I'm ready to start dating again, but I'm a little worried about the rules of bringing new women around. Got any tips about how to bring up the topic with the girls? —D. F., Oregon

You're smart to be concerned. Often, parents forget that while they may be ready go on with their lives, their children may need more time. Children of divorce are often vulnerable, sometimes fearful of abandonment., and have had to adjust to watching a parent leave, moving to new living and school situations, and leaving them feeling guilty that somehow the divorce was their fault. Having a parent's attention and time taken over by a new person can increase the fear of being cast aside, especially if it's the custodial parent.

So, how does a parent fill the void in his heart without leaving a void in his kids' lives? Start by reassuring your children that you love them, and

"I like you and want to get to know you," you'll be fine. Allow them to question you, put you through challenges, without complaining. Trust me: They'll ask Dad if you complained—if he says, "No, she thought you guys were great," they'll be disarmed. Always remember, you'll never sub for Mom, and you shouldn't try, but you *could* end up being a great older friend.

Bowling Green, KY: What is an acceptable amount of time to date someone before meeting his or her children? I have reiterating that the divorce is not their fault. Explain that you are going to start dating because it's natural for an adult to want to be in a loving relationship with another adult, but that doesn't mean they will be replaced.

Once you've prepped the girls for what's to come, constant communication and common sense are the keys to keeping everyone happy. Do introduce your children to your new "friends" on casual outings and encourage them to tell you what they think about them. (This will make them feel important and reinforces the idea that this person is an addition to *their* household, not a takeover.) Don't have your dates sleep over or display physical affection beyond holding hands, a hug, or a peck. And finally, just as you shouldn't expect your kids to fall instantly in love with someone just because *you* love them, you should also not expect to find the person of your dreams within the first few dates. A relationship is only as good as the time invested.

been dating a guy for four months and have only met one of his three children. He doesn't seem all that anxious for me to meet the other two, which concerns me, although I'm not really sure why.

DH: Don't be concerned—you two are still in a very early stage of your relationship. This guy sounds like a careful, concerned person, so if your relationship is lovely, don't worry about meeting the kids for another few months.

First Dates

Dublin, OH: I fear rejection. What do I do?

DH: Let me tell you, I hate rejection, too . . . but when it comes to dating, it's just part of the territory! That said, you need to get your self-esteem ready. Here's the mantra for you to repeat over and over again as you do get rejected: "Everyone—even famous, gorgeous people—faces rejection." Say to yourself, "Oh, well, that person didn't want me, but he doesn't know what he's missing . . . and there are about twenty million people I haven't met yet, with someone in there who will be my perfect catch!" Remember, just because you are wonderful, you may not find the person who appreciates *that kind of wonderful* right off the bat. Take rejection in stride, reset your focus, and keep moving forward.

Atchison, KS: I need to tell a guy I like him, but I'm too shy. Help!

DH: Being shy is so hard, mostly because there's that feeling that *no one else* feels as uncomfortable in social situations as you do! That couldn't be further from the truth. Did you know that most people who are social dynamos often get tongue-tied or shy around people they really like?

That said, what you have to do is psyche yourself up. Remind yourself that anything worthy is a risk worth taking. If you two are already on a talking basis, say, "I was thinking about seeing a movie this weekend—got any suggestions about what I should see?" Get him talking about what he's seen, and what he's dying to see, and then say, "Wanna go together?" *If* he comes up with a billion excuses why he can't, drop it, and consider trying again at another time. If nothing happens at that point, it's time to set your sights on someone else.

Boca Raton, FL: I've been friends for a few years with this girl who's a waitress at my favorite Chinese eatery. She's always delighted to see me when I come in to eat, but I wasn't quite sure how I felt about her, so I stayed neutral and kept things on a friendly basis. I sent her some flowers a few weeks ago, and she was thrilled. I have the feeling that she was waiting for me to ask her out. How should I handle this?

DH: You were brave enough to send flowers, you sense she's waiting for you to ask her out. . . . Dude! Call her at the restaurant, and say, "I know you're at work, so I won't keep you long— but would you like to go out one night?" I'm betting she'll say yes, so be sure you have a plan in place before you call.

Philadelphia, PA: How do you suggest that a man first approach a woman whom he is attracted to?

DH: You'll know if a woman is interested because she'll smile back at you when you catch her eye and smile at her. If this happens, just go up, say hello, and introduce yourself. Ask her to dance or if she'd like something to drink and get her talking. Trust me, if she already likes you, she'll help the conversation along.

Getting Back on the Scene

New York, NY: I was in a lonely marriage for eight years and have been divorced for two. I am not seeing anyone and doubt that

I will ever meet the love of my life. I enjoy the holiday season, but it also makes me lonely as I watch families spending time together. I feel I am waiting for some good times that may never come!

DH: Stop waiting, and get yourself out into circulation! Try online dating, or take a new class, or try volunteering—anything that will make you realize just how valuable a person you are, and that gets you out there meeting new people! Remember, you were married for eight years and had someone by your side, yet you were "lonely." Many seemingly happy couples that you are comparing yourself to may actually be in that same boat. *You*, my dear, had the guts to move on, knowing you deserved something better. Don't let the holiday schmaltz stop that fire!

Fort Worth, TX: Life is good. My career is dynamite, and my relationship with my young son is superb. But I can't, no matter what I do, seem to find anyone I want to date for long. I am forty— is everyone left a freak?

DH: You're in a terrific position to date: Life is *good*, and you're *not needy*! I suggest: 1) taking your son to volunteer at some organization once a week to expand your friendship circle, and give him a wonderful experience in helping others; and 2) checking out a secure online dating site like Match.com, where you can enter the qualifications you're looking for and basically go shopping (without ever leaving your house) for someone worthy of shaving your legs for that night. While I do agree that the older you get, the more baggage many people carry, I don't think all is lost; after all, *you* sound like a great catch, and I'm betting there're lots of other great ones out there just looking to connect.

Washington, DC: I've been single for more than a year. Where are all the "nice" men? The ones I meet all seem to think I want to give it up right then and there!

DH: Trust me, there are *tons* of nice men out there! Unfortunately, many of them are not packaged quite as slickly as the bad boys. Resolve to give someone who's not necessarily your usual type a chance—or go on an Internet dating adventure, or scan your local paper for neighborhood events and go just for the heck of it. In other words, get yourself out there and make yourself known to as many guys as possible. The odds are on your side that you may just meet someone when you least expect it.

Orlando, FL: Several months ago my two-year relationship ended. I have had enough time to adjust, and feel ready to get back on the horse. However, I seem to have lost the desire or skills to find someone new. The bar scene isn't the place, and I work at home so that doesn't help. Where does one get their groove back?

DH: I agree—the bar scene isn't one of the greatest places to meet a potential significant other. However, because dating is such a phenom today, there are so many other options:

Singles Stuff: Speed dating, singles cruises, or get-togethers.

Magazine Personals and the Internet: Responding to—and placing—personals ads.

Fate Dates: Keeping yourself open to meeting guys anywhere and everywhere.

I always encourage singles to volunteer—that way, your mind is off *your* issues as you help others, and you meet great people with *huge hearts.*

The most important thing is that you get out of the house, away from TV, and out into the great, wide open—hang with friends, take classes that interest you, try activities that you've always wanted to excel in. All of these things will get you out there, meeting wonderful people. Good luck!

Washington, DC: I am a twenty-five-year-old female and have never been in a serious relationship. The longest I've dated someone is two months. Is there something wrong with me? I feel developmentally delayed and almost ashamed of my lack of experience.

DH: At twenty-five, I was in an every-three-months dating jag. I never, *ever* thought I'd find someone who wanted a committed relationship. Guys at this age are incredibly hard to pin down unless they are established. Keep dating and stop worrying about past non-success. Trust me: You *will* eventually find a guy willing to commit . . . but don't, unless he meets all your Non-Negotiables: He respects you, cares for you, honors and loves you, shares your goals, and supports your dreams.

Dating Dilemmas

Glen Burnie, MD: I have been dating a guy for several months now. I thought he may be "the one" until religion came up. I am Catholic; he is a born-again Christian. Now, my friends are telling me there is a great possibility of problems in the future. They tell me a couple should be pretty similar in the religion area, and that if not, it can cause huge problems. Is this true? (My guy has some-times criticized Catholics in front of me.) Is this a red flag?

DH: Religion isn't a red flag unless both of you are very in-volved in your faith, particularly if you plan on one day having kids. Very often, couples of different faiths (who are very involved in their religion) argue and split over issues about what faith to raise the kids. If you two are getting serious, pick a night to discuss the pros, cons, ins, outs, and commitments involved. If you both cannot compromise on this issue, then you may have to reconsider this relationship.

Thunder Bay, Ontario: It seems that I am perceived as an overly friendly person and, to be honest, I am. Too often people see friendly as flirty, and I am concerned about the image that creates. Although I am single, I am not especially looking for someone and wondered if you have some tips on avoiding the "over friendly" way of conversing.

DH: The best thing you can do is avoid touching. Many warm, friendly people reach out and touch a person's arm or hand when they talk. The breaking down of physical barriers can some-times lead the other person to think there's more to your actions than merely wanting to connect on a friendly level.

Memphis, TN: Any "guy-catching" tips?

DH: I say, keep yourself open to new experiences, go new places with friends, get out and get social. The most fun way to meet a guy is when you aren't getting dressed and going to a bar to catch one—instead, you're taking lessons for a sport or hobby you love, or volunteering generously, and running into a guy who shares those interests (I call those "fate dates").

Seattle, WA: I have been reading your *USA WEEKEND* columns and "chats" for a while now, and when people ask about meeting others, you send them to do some volunteer work and meet people that way. I think that's a great way; however, I'm only twenty-two, just out of college, and moved here very recently (couple of months ago). I feel like the people who volunteer are mostly a lot older than me. Any other suggestions?

DH: You bring up a good point, and I'm glad you did! Many volunteers *are* older, mostly because they have a more structured schedule. I've noticed that when it comes to environmental issues, the crowd is about your age . . . perhaps that would be a great place for you to start. You may also want to head over to your local hospital to see if you can volunteer time with kids—you'll be surrounded by many young doctors-in-training! There's also volunteering for local politicians—lots of young people looking for careers in politics start off working at grassroots levels.

Milwaukee, WI: What are the signs of a healthy relationship?

DH: Laughter, honesty, communication . . . making out on the couch just for the sheer joy of being in each other's arms, with no expectation of it going any further . . . being able to fight fairly and forgive wholeheartedly . . . you both always look for an opportunity to surprise each other . . . A healthy relationship lifts you up and enhances you as a person.

Relationship Q & A

I can't stand how this sounds: The man I have been dating for over a year is starting to hint around about marriage. My problem: he's not as "smart" as I am. He's charming and funny, but he just doesn't have what I guess you'd call "book smarts." Am I being a total intellectual snob?
—H. N., Texas

It's good that you are really taking the hints about marriage to heart and are starting to think about whether or not this guy is right for you. But, if you're allowing lack of "book smarts" to override all the other wonderful qualities this man may have, then you are definitely more "snob" than smart! An intellectual man who doesn't treat you with love, respect, and consideration is definitely inferior to a not-so-well-read man who possesses all of those qualities and more.

That said, do continue to evaluate your man's life partner potential, but on five different levels: intellectually, emotionally, spiritually, physically, and financially. Start by asking yourself what it is about him that kept you interested for over a year, and don't hesitate to ask trusted friends for their thoughts. If they say that they've never seen you happier in a relationship, take that into consideration. Just keep in mind that this guy is ready to get married, so if you don't think he's the one for you, you'll need to be honest and end things now. Want to continue the relationship? Love grows stronger when you learn from each other: Introduce him to some of the books you love, and allow him to share his passions with you. You may be surprised at how much *you* don't know!

Scottsdale, AZ: I met a woman about a year ago who lives in another state. She came to town last weekend, and we hit it off wonderfully. She's everything I could possibly want in a girl, and that threw me off-balance. We went out to a couple of nightclubs, and I went into macho overdrive, basically acting like (and telling her) that I could have any other woman there. She got upset, but in the end we were together and happy. Should I explain to her that I was just feeling insecure, and that I'm not really that woman-crazy guy she was with that night? How should I go about forming a relationship with this ideal person, considering we live in different states?

DH: I've gotten this letter from a *lot* of guys . . . the letter that says that he met the woman of his dreams, and basically *sabotaged* the night by trying too hard to prove to her that he was a much-wanted stud-muffin, which, of course, is something that many men *think* impresses a woman, but doesn't. My answer is don't beat yourself up, but do give yourself a little kick and make a promise not to do this again.

The woman worthy of your love wants a man who has eyes for her, and makes her feel special. If she's still talking to you, I want you to actually say to her, "By the way . . . that night you were over? Just wanted you to know . . . if I was a little over the top, it was only because I like you so much, I wanted to show off for you, because, I don't know if you know this, guys think that showing how many women *want* you shows their worth. But now that I think about how upset I made you, I realize that was stupid."

In the meantime, be the guy she can brag about to her friends: "Yes, he may be long-distance, but he wrote me the most wonderful letter—yes, actually wrote it in *pen*, not an e-mail! And I love how he can bare his feelings for me. . . ."

And be phone smart: Only call her when you can pay full attention to what she says. If she mentions something important like, "I have my realtor's licensing test tomorrow," *send flowers*! Or, if on a budget, be sure to send a card: "I know you aced that test—you are wonderful."

Nashville, TN: What do you think of the theory that opposites attract? I've dated only two women in the past few years. One had nothing in common with me, and the other has very similar tastes. I enjoyed dating both of them, and the only difference seems to be that I had to compromise a lot more with the opposite one. But isn't compromise part of a relationship?

DH: Sure, "opposites attract," but it's what two people have in common that keeps couples together. My advice: When you feel like being with someone is all about how much you compromise, that person is *not* for you. Continue dating the one whom you feel most comfortable with.

Bowling Green, KY: Why do some guys come on really strong at first and then back way off? I've had this happen several times and still can't figure out why.

DH: It's so unfair, isn't it? The guy comes on strong. Encouraged, we react in a very open, "I want you, too" manner. The guy backs off, thinking *we* are the ones rushing into things! Your best bet: When a guy starts talking about your future grandchildren on the first date, slow him down. Say, "We'll see where this goes one date at a time!" This makes the guy think he has to work a little harder—something his "hunter" ego enjoys.